Military a [illegible] Israel's Coming Wars

ISRAEL'S *FUTURE* WARS

MILITARY AND POLITICAL ASPECTS OF ISRAEL'S COMING WARS

EHUD EILAM

Westphalia Press
An Imprint of the Policy Studies Organization
Washington, DC
2016

ISRAEL'S FUTURE WARS

Westphalia Press
An imprint of Policy Studies Organization
1527 New Hampshire Ave., NW
Washington, D.C. 20036
info@ipsonet.org

ISBN-10: 1-63391-506-9
ISBN-13: 978-1-63391-506-0

Cover and interior design by Jeffrey Barnes
jbarnesbook.design

Daniel Gutierrez-Sandoval, Executive Director
PSO and Westphalia Press

Updated material and comments on this edition
can be found at the Westphalia Press website:
www.westphaliapress.org

Contents

Glossary

APC – armored personnel carrier
CFR – The Council on Foreign Relations
CSIS – Center for Strategic International Studies
CW – Chemical weapons
Gulf – the Persian/Arab Gulf
IAF – Israeli Air Force
IDF – Israel Defense Forces
IED – Improvised explosive device
INSS – Institute for National Security Studies
MB – Muslim Brotherhood
MFO – Multinational force and observers (in Sinai)
PA – Palestinian Authority
PLO – Palestine Liberation Organization
UAV – Unmanned air vehicle

Preface

This research examines Israel's possible future wars in the upcoming years. It analyzes the strategic background and the nature of operations of those wars and concentrates on feasible future battlefields of Israel in Iran, Lebanon, Syria, the Gaza Strip, the West Bank, and Sinai.

An Israeli strike against Iran's nuclear sites could instigate a war between Israel and Iran and/or the Hezbollah in Lebanon. Existing tension with Syria could induce Israel to collaborate with Syrian armed groups against Islamic radicals in the Golan Heights. In the Gaza Strip, friction between Israel and the Hamas might result in a confrontation. Israel might also collide with Palestinians in the West Bank as part of a struggle with the Palestinian Authority (PA). Another confrontation might occur between Israel and Egypt because of the unrest in the Sinai Peninsula.

Since Israel was established in 1948, its basic national security concern has been deterring Arabs from starting a high-intensity war and winning such a confrontation if it happens. In 1948–1949, 1956, 1967, 1973, and 1982, Israel's main enemies were Arab states such as Egypt, Syria, Jordan, and Iraq. As part of the Arab–Israeli conflict, Israel had to take into account major strategic constraints. Paramount among them was the huge gap between Israel and the Arabs in favor of the latter, in terms of the size of population, land and natural resources. Israel also lacked strategic depth in key sectors. During the wars, Israel fought alone except for 1956, when Israel joined France and Britain against Egypt.[1] Israel has also enjoyed the support of the United States, mostly from the late 1960s.[2]

In October 2015, Lt. Col. Alon Paz, who served as a strategist in the IDF's Strategic Planning Division, claimed that preparing for future wars has to do with "setting clear and adaptive political objectives that resonate with broader goals for the competition; discussing the linkages between military (and other) means and political ends; establishing entry and exit strategies when military conflict occurs; engaging in post-conflict planning and multidimensional war planning orchestrated with the various national lines of effort; phasing; requirements for plan adjustments; and adaptive planning for limited challenges."[3]

This research does not deal with the various political, social, economic, cultural, moral, and legal matters concerning Israel and the IDF that could possibly affect the next war,[4] nor does it focus on the overall national security policy of Israel, and its conflict with Iran and/or the Arabs. The focus here is on certain aspects such as the calculations leading to an Israeli attack on Iran's nuclear project, Hezbollah's constraints regarding starting a war against Israel, Israel's involvement in Syria, and the Israeli dilemma regarding a conceivable conquest of the Gaza Strip.

The Israeli military doctrine is based on striving for a fast victory by taking the initiative. A case in point occurred in 1956 and 1967 when Israel launched a massive land and air attack deep into Arab territory. The operational aims were to destroy Arab forces and to capture the vital areas. The IDF buildup relies on land and air forces with relatively small regular manpower, which means that most of the troops come from the reserves.[5] The IDF developed and tested its doctrine and buildup over the years, and in spite of various blunders and setbacks, its achievements in combat made it a force to be reckoned with.

In recent decades, Israel conducted hybrid confrontations: against the Hezbollah in 2006[6] and the Hamas, such as in 2008–2009 and 2014. Israel also dealt with prolonged low-intensity wars in the West Bank and the Gaza Strip in 1987–1993 and 2000–2005.[7] Although Israel's top security challenge until the 1990s was a high-intensity war against Arab states, a future war might be against a state and/or a nonstate organization.

This research laid emphasis on certain operational patterns that deal with each front, such as the kind of forces that might attack in Iran, the way Israel might destroy rockets in Lebanon, the military vulnerability of the Gaza Strip, the manner in which Israel might collaborate with Syrian rebels, and so on. Another focus is on combat actions of land and air forces, mostly bombardments and maneuvers such as urban warfare.

The nonfiction literature on Israel's national security usually does not evaluate future wars. This research strives to show how past and current events, developments, etc. might influence the next war.

It includes hundreds of endnotes supporting my ideas. The information and references to books, articles, etc. are always incorporated into the text itself, in a way that does not disrupt the flow of reading. The only purpose of the endnotes is to reveal the details of the source. The links appearing in the endnotes were last accessed in August 2016, a few months before the book was published.

I hold an M.A. and a Ph.D. degree in my field of expertise: Israel's national strategy and military doctrine. I have been carrying out research in those subjects for more than 20 years. I worked for a few years as a researcher for Israeli Ministry of Defense, as a private contractor. This book is a completely personal project and is not a part of any research I did for the Israeli Ministry of Defense. This research expresses my personal views and does not necessarily represent the opinions of others. I have worked on this research in Israel and also where I now reside in the United States. For readers with questions, comments, etc. about the book please write to me at: Ehudei2014@gmail.com.

Introduction

Israel has been fighting wars since it was established in 1948. This research is about Israel's upcoming wars, that is, confrontations that might take place in the near future in Iran, Lebanon, Syria, the Gaza Strip, the West Bank, and Sinai. Most of those collisions would be hybrid or low-intensity wars.

The order of the chapters is based on Israel's strategic priorities, determined through following political and military leadership announcements, reading open reports about IDF preparations for war, and evaluating the potential military capability of Israel's foes, currently and in the future.

Chapter One discusses the conflict between Israel and Iran. If Iran breaches the July 2015 agreement regarding its nuclear program, Israel might attack Iran. Israel could bomb Iran's oil industry in order to cripple its economy and perhaps undermine the regime, or at least make it difficult for Iran to finance its nuclear project. Yet, ramifications on the global economy would be such that Israel would probably restrict itself to attacking the Iranian nuclear infrastructure solely. Israel could use several forces, mostly from the Israeli Air Force (IAF). Iran might retaliate with its long-range missiles or show restraint and wait for a better opportunity to take its revenge.

Chapter Two explores Israel and the Lebanese nonstate organization Hezbollah, which is currently busy in fighting inside Syria. If Israel attacks Iran's nuclear sites, the pro-Iranian Hezbollah might clash with Israel, although it is not certain. Hezbollah has up to 150,000 rockets that cover almost every spot in Israel. If the Hezbollah opens fire, Israel would launch a massive air, land, and sea offensive aimed at destroying as many rockets as possible. This collision might be more intense and costly for both sides than the last confrontation between them in 2006.

Chapter Three treats Israel's Syrian front. If the Assad regime collapses, Syria's land and skies might turn into a battlefield between Israel and its foes like the Hezbollah and Iran. Either way Israel might develop its ties with Syrian rebels and minorities like the Druze as part of securing the Golan Heights against Islamic radicals.

Chapter Four concentrates mostly on the Hamas in the Gaza Strip, which has been clashing with Israel for more than two decades. In case of another round, the Hamas might be left without allies because of the rift between itself and Iran and the hostility it inspires in Arab states like Egypt. Israel would consider conquering part or all of the Gaza Strip, with or without cooperation with the PA. The IDF might penetrate the Gaza Strip from land, air, and sea. In addition, there might be another collision between Israel and the Palestinians in the West Bank, starting with demonstrations and ending in a low-intensity war.

Chapter Five discusses a possible clash between Israel and Egypt. The former might have to run a low-intensity war in Sinai against guerrilla and terror groups, a struggle that in the worst-case scenario might deteriorate into a high-intensity war between Israel and Egypt. Such a confrontation could be comprehensive, including a fight for air superiority.

Notes

1 David Ben Gurion, *Uniqueness and Destiny* (Tel Aviv: Ministry of Defense, 1972). Yigal Allon, *Curtain of Sand* (Tel Aviv: Hakibbutz Hameuchad, 1960). Avner Yaniv, *Politics and Strategy in Israel* (Tel Aviv: Sifriat Poalim, 1994). Israel Tal, *National Security* (Tel Aviv: Dvir, 1996). Michael L. Handel, *Israel's Political-Military Doctrine* (Harvard University Press, 1973).

2 Abraham Ben Zvi, *The United States and Israel—The Limits of the Special Relationship* (New York: Columbia University Press, 1993). Steven L. Spiegel, *The Other Arab-Israeli Conflict* (Chicago: The University of Chicago, 1985).

3 Alon Paz, "Transforming Israel's Security Establishment," The Washington Institute for Near East Policy, October 2015, http://www.washingtoninstitute.org/policy-analysis/view/transforming-

israels-security-establishment.

4 On those issues see for example: Amichai Cohen, and Stuart Cohen, *Israel's National Security Law* (New York: Routledge, 2011). Yagil Levy, *Who Governs the Military? Between Control of the Military and Control of Militarism* (Jerusalem: Eshkolot Library and Magnes University Press, 2010).

5 Avi Kober, *Military Decision in the Arab–Israeli Wars 1948–1982* (Tel Aviv: Ministry of Defense, 1995). Martin Van Creveld, *The Sword and the Olive—A Critical History of the Israeli Defence Force* (New York: Public Affairs, 1998). Dov Tamari, *The Armed Nation—The Rise and Decline of the Israel Reserve System* (Tel Aviv: Ministry of Defense, 2012).

Arial Levite, *Offense and Defense* (Tel Aviv: Hakibbutz Hameuchad, 1988). The Israel Defense Forces and Defense Establishment Archives (IDFA) 55/488/261. Edward Luttwak, and Dan Horowitz, *The Israeli Army* (New York: Harper and Row, 1975).

6 On the 2006 war see: Amos Harel, and Avi Issacharoff, *34 Days: Israel, Hezbollah, and the War in Lebanon* (New York: Palgrave Macmillan, 2008). Amir Rapaport, *Friendly Fire* (Tel Aviv: Ma'ariv Books, 2007). Shmuel Gordon, *The Second Lebanon War: Strategic Decisions and their Consequences* (Ben-Shemen, Israel: Modan, 2012).

7 On the 2000–05 war see: Amos Harel, and Avi Isacharoff, *The Seventh War* (Miskal: Yedioth Ahronoth Books and Chemed Books, 2004). Daniel Byman, *A High Price—the Triumphs and Failures of Israeli Counterterrorism* (Oxford University Press, 2011).

Uri Ben-Eliezer, *Old Conflict, New War: Israel's Politics Toward the Palestinians* (New York: Palgrave Macmillan, 2012).

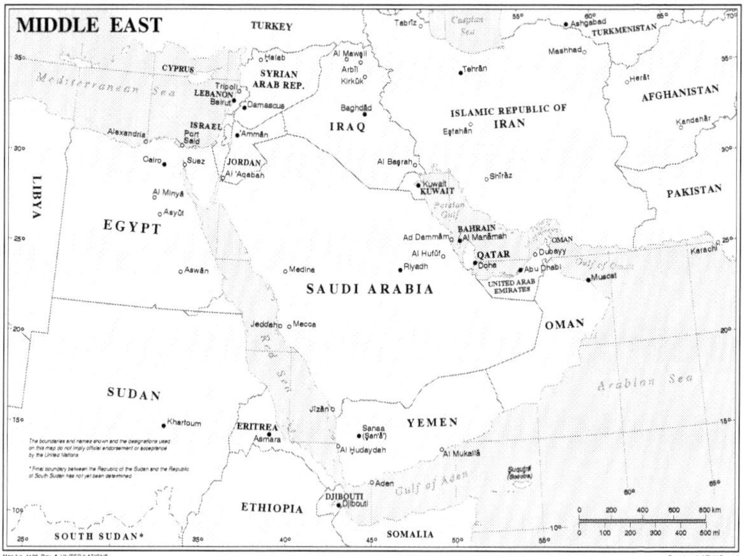

Map No. 4102 Rev. 8 UNITED NATIONS
November 2011

Department of Field Support
Cartographic Section

Map No. 3584 Rev. 2 UNITED NATIONS
January 2004

Department of Peacekeeping Operations
Cartographic Section

Chapter 1

An Israeli Attack on Iran

Israel and Iran have been engaged in a Cold War of sorts since the early 1980s. Iran's enhanced development of nuclear weapons may lead Israel to attack Iran's nuclear sites. If that happens, Iran might retaliate.

The Iranian approach toward Israel

Iran and Israel enjoyed a fruitful relationship until the late 1970s,[1] so much so that some Israelis envisioned producing a fighter jet together with Iran.[2] The Islamic Revolution in Iran in 1979 changed all that. Iran became locked in a bitter rivalry with Israel.[3] Many senior figures in Iran consider "Israel's very existence as illegitimate."[4] Iran's supreme leader, Ayatollah Ali Khamenei, has expressed his hatred for Israel numerous times.

There is some hope for coexistence between Iran and Israel. The two states—separated by >1,000 km—have no real reason to confront each other. There are no disputes over land or water, contrary to the problems between Israel and the Palestinians. There has never been a shooting war between Israel and Iran, just a 37-year-old multidimensional Cold War, manifested by direct clashes between Israel and pro-Iranian nonstate organizations (the Islamic Jihad, the Hamas, and the Hezbollah) and covert operations including cyberwarfare, assaults on Jewish and Israeli civilians around the world and the assassinations of Iranian nuclear scientists in Iran.

There is a direct line between the Old Persian Empire (550–330 BCE) and the Islamic Republic of Iran. Much has changed, but much has remained the same.[5] In comparison with the Old Persian

Empire, ancient Israel was tiny even at the peak of its territorial expansion. Similarly, Iran today has a lot more land, people and natural resources than Israel does. (For example, Israel is 22,072 km^2 while Iran is 1,648,195 km^2.) The fact that Israel now owns large amounts of natural gas doesn't change the balance of power between it and Iran. Although Israel is tiny, it has quite impressive military capabilities, conventional and nonconventional, as well as economic strength. Iran, striving for hegemony in the region, can't ignore Israel because it is too powerful. However, Israel is not intimidating enough to force Iran into tolerating its presence, as Iran does with other strong rivals around it, like Turkey. As location wise Israel is not under the shadow of Iran, it's harder for the latter to impose its will on Israel and vice versa. The Israeli Defence Force (IDF)'s achievements in wars are not that relevant due to the distance between Israel and Iran and the size of that country. Israel cannot coerce Iran into accepting Israel's right to exist.

Iran seeks to have pro-Iranian regimes in states in the Middle East.[6] From an Iranian perspective, it seems Israeli Jews should have the same status they had before their state was established, i.e., when they were subjected to foreign powers. Naturally, Iran does not wish for the return of the British mandate or any other Western power. Iran longs for the period in which Jews in the land of Israel were subordinate to an Islamic regime (the Ottoman Empire). Presently, Iran could accept an Arab government there in place of the Turks, preferably a pro-Iranian one. Thus, the Iranian regime can claim that it is not against the Jews in Israel, but only against their state.

The nuclear threat

On April 28, 2015, Mohammad Javad Zarif, Iran's foreign minister, claimed that Israel has 400 nuclear warheads.[7] According to non-Israeli sources, Israel has the Bomb. It's possible that Israel's military power, particularly its nuclear potential, may be one of the reasons that Iran is eager to get a hold of the Bomb or nuclear weapon capability.

Louis René Beres, Professor of political science, said in February 2016 that Israel "would do best to remain focused on maintaining more recognizably secure and penetration-capable nuclear retaliatory forces."[8] Israel, which opposes the Iranian regime and its policy, could also warn Iran, secretly or publicly, that it must comply with Israel's demands or else. In such a case, Iran would probably estimate that Israel was bluffing, i.e., would not use its nuclear weapons. On the other hand, one can assume that if Iran had nuclear weapons and Israel did not, Iran could coerce Israel into accepting Iran's demands. This is based not only on the difference between the two cultures but also on historical facts: Iran and its proxies have been attacking Israel and its people since the 1980s with methods that Israel has not used against Iran, such as suicide bombers and firing rockets on civilians.

If Iran eventually produces the Bomb, Israel might be seen as a state facing annihilation. This would be a major setback for the country in terms of foreign investments, immigration, and increment in its defense budget. Another ramification might be that pro-Iranian organizations like Hezbollah and radical Palestinian groups in the Gaza Strip such as the Islamic Jihad would be encouraged to provoke Israel by launching rockets at it, expecting Israel to think twice before retaliating, particularly with a massive operation, because Iran could back its proxies. However, it is doubtful whether Iran would risk a nuclear war against Israel in order to protect its protégés.

Israel has never used unconventional weapons against the Arab states and vice versa. In contrast, Arabs did use chemical weapons (CW) on other Arabs in Yemen in the 1960s and on non-Arab Muslims, such as the Kurds in Iraq and the Iranians, during the 1980s. Bashar al Assad also used CW against his Syrian population during the uprising against him. Those precedents in the Middle East might pave the way for Iran to use unconventional weapons against Israel.

Avi Primor, as the president of the Israel Council on Foreign Relations, commented in early 2014 on the Israeli approach toward Iran: "Many Israelis believe that they are not facing an entirely rational regime; therefore, they should not count on logical arguments such as the danger to Israel's neighbors or Israel's deterrent power, to dissuade the Iranians."[9] According to Jeffrey Herf, a professor in the department of history at the University of Maryland, "U.S. policymakers cannot assume that Iran will value its own survival more than it does the goal of eliminating the hated Jewish enemy."[10]

It is undoubtedly difficult to understand both the decision-making process and the actual goals of Iran. Since Israel has its own complicated decision-making constraints, according to Charles Freilich, a senior fellow at the Belfer Center of Harvard's Kennedy School of Government and a former deputy national security adviser in Israel,[11] each side is likely to be concerned about the other in this matter.

Still, Israel should be much more worried. It's a strange irony that Iran, which does not possess nuclear weapons, has been publicly provoking a state that is believed to have the Bomb. It seems that Iran does not care or perhaps does not believe that Israel actually possesses this deadly weapon and has accepted Israel's vague denials about holding the Bomb. If Iran behaves that way now, how would that regime act if it actually had nuclear weapons? Would there be a way for Israel to deter Iran?

Greg Thielmann, a senior fellow of the Arms Control Association, claimed in May 2014 that Iran's ballistic missiles should not be part of the nuclear program talks.[12] However, if Iran develops ballistic missiles capable of carrying a nuclear warhead and eventually obtains the Bomb, it will be a serious threat to Israel. Israel has its Arrow system to be used against such missiles, but it has never been tested in combat.

An Iranian plane with a nuclear cargo would be another problem.

Although it would be easier for Israel to intercept an Iranian plane than a missile, it would still be a major challenge. In a time of crisis between the two states, the Israeli Air Force (IAF) would be ready to prevent an Iranian aircraft from getting close enough to drop the Bomb on an Israeli target. However, in quieter times, when the IDF would not be on full alert, the danger to Israel would be much higher. Iran could also send several planes, only one of them with the Bomb, assuming that Israel might not be able to shoot down the aircraft that has the Bomb. Due to the distance between Israel and Iran, the latter might refuel its planes in Iraq, which is closer to Israel and partly under strong Iranian influence. Another Iranian ally, Assad, might allow Iran to refuel in Syria, which has a border with Israel. Iran could also send its planes on a suicide mission, with enough fuel to reach Israel from Iran but not enough to return. There are numerous possibilities, and considering the drastic ramifications of a nuclear attack on Israel, it is clear why the latter wishes to avoid such a risk to begin with.

Was Israel about to attack Iran in 2014–2015?

Israel, both the government and many of its people, is firmly convinced that Iran's intentions toward Israel are hostile and evil, and there has been no trust in the Iranian announcements that it does not wish to produce nuclear weapons. From Iranian declarations, it is quite clear that Iran wishes to wipe Israel off the map. From Israeli announcements, it is obvious that Israel accepts the right of Iran to exist but seeks to get rid of the current Iranian regime and/or its nuclear program. Iran's declared goals cannot be accomplished if it does not obtain a nuclear weapon or the ability to send it all the way to its target. Israel cannot bring about regime change in Iran; it can only attack and cause a delay in the Iranian nuclear program, hoping that meanwhile the regime falls due to internal developments.

Syria gave up its nuclear option after its reactor was destroyed by Israel in September 2007. Following the invasion of Iraq in 2003 and the pain of sanctions, another Arab country, Libya, agreed to dismantle its nuclear program. Iran too postponed its nuclear project. This indicates that sometimes using force in the Middle East can, directly or not, convince states in that region to change their nuclear policy.

Matthew Kroenig claimed in 2014 that if diplomacy fails and Iran "ramps up its nuclear program," there would be about "2 to 12 months to solve the Iranian nuclear challenge."[13] Talks between Iran and world powers, aimed at reaching an accord, continued in 2014. In spite of that, Israel's defense minister, Moshe Ya'alon, ordered the IDF to go on preparing for a raid in Iran.[14] In late April 2014, Brig. Gen. (Ret.) Yaakov Amidror, Israel's former national security adviser, expressed his strong reservations about the emerging agreement.[15] A month later, Emily Landau, an expert in the field, stated that as long as the negotiations continue, the military option is not on the table. According to Landau, the Israeli references to a potential attack were made possibly to pressure Iran as part of the talks.[16]

In the Council on Foreign Relations' annual Preventive Priorities Survey for 2015, 2,200 government officials, academics and foreign policy experts ranked as "moderate" the likelihood that there would be "renewed threat of Israeli military strikes against Iran as a result of a breakdown in nuclear negotiations and/or clear evidence of intent to develop a nuclear weapons capability."[17]

On February 11, 2015, following talks between world powers and Iran about the country's nuclear project, Israel's intelligence affairs minister, Yuval Steinitz, warned, "All options are still on the table ... we never limited Israel's right of self-defense because of some diplomatic constraints."[18] Maj. Gen. (Ret.) Amos Yadlin is a former head of the IDF intelligence directorate. In March 2015, in regard to an Israeli military option against Iran, he argued that "it is doable."[19] Efraim Inbar, director of the Begin-Sadat Center for Strategic Studies, claimed in April 2015 that Israel is willing to accomplish this mission.[20]

In May 2014, Zaki Shalomis, a member of the research staff at the Institute for National Security Studies (INSS), a major think tank in Israel, argued that it looks as if "the negative U.S. attitude to an independent Israeli military strike against Iran, in and of itself, would not deter the government of Prime Minister Netanyahu from unilateral military action if and when it realized that this was its only remaining option for preventing Iran from going nuclear."[21] The same could be said following the establishment of Netanyahu's new government in May 2015, which is more right-wing than the former one.

On June 16, 2015, IDF's chief of general staff, Lt. Gen. Gadi Eizenkot, said that Iran's nuclear project is the greatest threat Israel faces, one that would occupy the IDF intelligence directorate and the IAF in the upcoming years.[22] On June 25, 2015, Prime Minister Benjamin Netanyahu said to newly graduated pilots and navigators that Iran's effort to gain a nuclear weapon is the biggest danger that Israel faces. He added that the IAF plays a major role in defending Israel. This announcement was considered "an implicit threat to Iran."[23] It meant that the IAF should be ready to strike Iran.

On July 14, 2015, following the agreement with Iran, former Israeli prime minister Ehud Barak said that Israel should keep the military option.[24] In his speech at the UN on October 1, 2015, Prime Minister Netanyahu said, "Israel will not allow Iran to break in, to sneak in or to walk in to the nuclear weapons club ... no one should question Israel's determination to defend itself against those who seek our destruction."[25] In early January 2016, an IDF general said that the IDF does not intend to reduce its "current capabilities for Iran," in spite of the nuclear deal with Iran.[26] Israel fears that Iran could continue with its nuclear program, despite the limitations imposed by the agreement, while hoping for a shift in its favor, such as a rift between Western powers that would allow Iran to breach the agreement and rush forward with its nuclear program. In such a situation, Israel might attack Iran.

If the United States does not give Israel the go-ahead, officially or not, and Israel attacks Iran anyway, it may significantly affect the American approach to Israel on the day after. Depending on the Iranian response, Israel might need quite a lot of help from its American patron. The United States might use this aid as leverage to force Israel to accept the American position in other cases, such as the Palestinian issue. Nonetheless, if Israel believes that there is no other choice but to attack Iran alone, then uncertainty about the American policy after the raid might be seen as a risk worth taking.

Would Israel attack the Iranian oil industry or leadership?

As to the main targets, "Iran ranks 18th among the biggest states, geographically. Its nuclear sites are geographically dispersed: The Natanz fuel enrichment plant is 130 miles southeast of Tehran. The Fordow uranium enrichment facility near Qom, identified in September 2009, is southwest of the Iranian capital. The Arak heavy water plant is about 150 miles south of Tehran. The Isfahan nuclear technology research center is in central Iran, 210 miles south of Tehran. The Karaj radioactive storage facility is 100 miles northwest of Tehran. The Bushehr reactor is in the Gulf, >500 miles from Tehran. The Parchin weapons development complex, which may also be a nuclear weapons development site, is located 19 miles southeast of Tehran."[27] There might be other objectives as well.

In October 1967, Egypt sank an Israeli destroyer. Israel retaliated by shelling Egypt's oil refineries.[28] In the 1973 war, Syrian infrastructure, including oil facilities, was bombed by the IAF as a response to Syrian rockets hitting the north of Israel.

In October 2013, Amos Yadlin mentioned that the Iranian oil industry and gas pipelines could be attacked if Iran retaliates fiercely, following a raid on its nuclear sites.[29]

Israel could also attack Iran's oil industry instead of storming the nuclear sites, which would be a major blow to the Iranian regime, since a large part of its revenues comes from oil. Without this financial source, the Iranian government would find it very difficult to afford the nuclear program and pay for basic expenses including subsidies, which would cause unrest that might topple the regime.

Iran could fortify oil sites, which would be quite a demanding and expensive task, considering their number and size. The oil infrastructure would remain very vulnerable also, since it is in the west of Iran, within striking range of Israeli aircraft, F-15I and F-16I, but then Iran and/or Hezbollah could fire on Israel's oil refineries in the city of Haifa.

An Israeli strike on Iranian oil sites and a possible Iranian response blocking the Strait of Hormuz could cause a sharp rise in the price of oil, and if high costs continue for a long time Israel would be blamed for hurting the world economy. This consideration, and other possible ramifications of an Israeli attack on the Iranian oil industry, may keep this option only as retribution for a severe Iranian attack against Israel.

If Israel mentioned that threat, it could cause Iran to send units like anti-aircraft batteries to protect oil facilities at the expense of defending nuclear sites. Also, during an attack on Iran's nuclear infrastructure, a diversion toward oil facilities could confuse and divert Iranian fighters to defend the wrong objectives. The Israeli assumption might be that the consequences of such a deception—a false threat on Iran's oil industry—would not be too damaging, not even to the global oil market.

Over the years, Israel has killed Arab leaders of guerrilla and terror groups,[30] mostly Palestinian ones. Saddam Hussein also became a target after he launched missiles at Israel in 1991. In 1992, there was an exercise by an elite Israeli unit aiming to assassinate Saddam Hussein, but the drill ended in an accident, with five Israeli soldiers killed by friendly fire. It was a rare case in which Israel planned to get rid of a leader of an Arab state by killing him.

Israel usually avoided such an approach although sometimes it hoped that defeating Arabs in wars would bring regime change in their countries. Yet this concept did not prove itself in cases such as Egypt's Gamal Abdel Nasser in 1956 and 1967.

During a raid on Iran, the IAF could target high-ranking officials.[31] Some of Iran's top brass and senior political figures reiterated or at least supported their state's proclaimed intention of annihilating Israel. The latter could attack Iranian leaders, but wiping them out would be a tall order, particularly if the goal was to kill them all in one coordinated strike. Some might survive and become more determined to develop the Bomb in order to deter or even attack Israel.

Killing Iranian leaders would expose Israel's senior figures in both the government and the IDF to decapitation. Instead of an actual assassination, Israel could try to intimidate Iranian leaders, but there doesn't seem to be much of a chance to convince them to moderate their declarations and certainly not to change their minds about Israel or about building the Bomb.

Israeli forces that could attack Iran

An Israeli raid on Iran's nuclear sites could demand the dispatching of about 100 aircraft.[32] They would include tankers, for air refueling, all the way to Iran and back.[33] The IAF does not possess long-range strategic bombers like the B-2, which has a range of about 11,000 km. Israel has only fighter bombers such as the F-15I with a much smaller range, almost 4,500 km. The shortest route to Iran is over Jordan and Iraq. Flying there would save fuel and reduce the probability of early spotting by Iran, which is essential since such a mission involves so many planes.

At the beginning of the Iran–Iraq war in 1980, Iran had more and better aircraft than those of its foe.[34] The Iranian air force has been in decline in recent years.[35] It has F-14s and MIG-29s, but they are not much of a match for Israel's F-15I and F-16I. Yet, according to classic roles of air warfare, the IAF might prefer to destroy Iran's planes in their airfields, on the ground, where they are helpless. Iran might have enough time to scramble its fighters before they are trapped in their bases. Iranian air crews would enjoy home advantages such as additional fuel for air-to-air combat. Israeli fighter bombers, being faster and smaller than Israel's command and control planes, would have more chances to survive against both Iranian fighters and anti-aircraft fire.

Iran upgraded its air defense in September 2015, when it claimed it had assimilated two long-range radars, one of which was supposed to have a range of 1,000 km.[36] In 2016, Iran got the Russian S-300PMU-1 anti-aircraft missile, not the most modern version of that system. Yet it could "detect up to 100 aerial targets simultaneously at a 300 km range, and engage 6 of them." The range of its anti-aircraft missiles is 150 km. It would "significantly improve Iran's air-defense capability once it eventually enters service. To effectively cover such a large country, however, Iran will still need to integrate the S-300s, with its modified S-200 and Raad surface-to-air missiles, and perhaps with the Bavar-373, a system that is claimed to be under development in Iran loosely based on the S-300 design."[37] Iran also has old anti-aircraft missile batteries such as the HAWK and SA-2, which are quite familiar to the IAF, also since the latter has had its own HAWK since the mid-1960s. The IAF, by using cyber and electronic warfare and air bombardments, might neutralize the Iranian air defense. Unmanned air vehicles (UAV), a field where Israel has quite a worldwide reputation, would contribute their share by gathering intelligence, attacking objectives, etc.

The IAF has bunker buster bombs such as the GBU-28, but they are not powerful enough to crack some of Iran's highly protected nuclear sites. Therefore, the IAF requires the massive ordnance penetrator (MOP), which was made and upgraded by the United States so it could do the job in Iran. Israel needs its American patron to provide it not only with the MOP but also with the B-52, to carry that huge bomb. Israel should at least get the MOP. Even without the B-52, the IAF might manage to put and to drop the MOP from its C-130, a transport plane. In the skies of Iran, the B-52/C-130 would face a serious risk from Iranian antiaircraft fire, but the IAF might be able to suppress it for enough time to accomplish the mission. In the past, the IAF conducted other kinds of dangerous and complicated operations.

Israel could hit Iran's nuclear sites with its Jericho long-range surface-to-surface missiles, carrying conventional warheads. Launching missiles over Arab states on their way to Iran would save jeopardizing air crews and their aircraft and might be more convenient politically than dispatching planes through Arab skies. However, Israel's long-range missiles with a conventional warhead may not penetrate Iranian protection and destroy the targets. For that Israel might have to fire hundreds of long-range missiles. Israel would rather keep its Jericho missiles as strategic arsenal for its nuclear option.

On May 5, 2015, Moshe Ya'alon said that Israel "might take certain steps that we believe ... in order to defend ourselves." He referred to U.S. president Harry Truman, who dropped the Bomb on Japan in 1945. Ya'alon then added that there is time for Israel to decide.[38] In this sense Israel could launch its Jericho missiles with nuclear warheads against Iranian nuclear facilities.[39] It might be necessary to crack the heavy protection of some nuclear sites. In past wars the IDF managed to handle its challenges solely with conventional forces, even during its darkest hours in the 1973 war. It could, however, be argued that if stopping Iran from producing the Bomb is so important and it could not be done with conventional methods, Israel could consider using nuclear weapons for that crucial task.

In 2009, an Israeli submarine crossed through the Suez Canal into the Red Sea.[40] This kind of vessel in the Israeli navy is supposed to carry missiles with a nuclear warhead that have a range of 1,500 km.[41] The missiles could be launched from the Red Sea and maybe even closer to Iran. However, Egypt—much as it opposes Iran having nuclear weapons—might not want to aggravate Iran by letting Israeli military vessels cross the Suez Canal as part of a strike on Iran. Israel, for obvious reasons of surprise, would avoid updating Egypt about its real intentions when sending its submarines through the Suez Canal, and after the strike on Iran, Israel could deny that its submarines took part in it. Still, this could cause a serious crisis between Israel and Egypt and therefore leaves Israeli submarines with the option of firing missiles from the Mediterranean Sea. That, however, presents the problem of range, because from that geographical point Israel might not be able to reach every target in Iran.

Israeli Special Forces, who have gained vast experience in daring operations over the years, could participate in the raid on Iran. In some cases, such as the rescue of Jewish hostages on July 4, 1976, in Entebbe, Uganda, they were sent thousands of kilometers away from Israel. They could reach Iran with C-130 transport planes, which could land on improvised runways and take vehicles with them. Israel's crack outfits could collect intelligence before the attack, direct air bombs to their targets, and conduct damage assessment after the raid.[42] Those units could be the one for "target designation (Sayeret Shaldag/Unit 5101) and for real-time bomb damage assessment (Unit 5707)."[43]

Israeli Elite forces might also storm nuclear sites or other objectives as part of securing the success of the raid. They might manage to infiltrate into Iranian facilities, pretending to be Iranians by sending Israeli troops who look Iranian and speak the language. Iranian Jews living in Israel could help. The Jews in Iran itself might not participate in an attack in Iran, fearing retribution against their community, but Iranian Kurds who oppose the Iranian regime might assist in this matter.

Conducting a sudden attack on Iran

In 2007, Israel took a huge risk striking the Syrian nuclear reactor, for Syria could have retaliated with a war, including firing missiles at the Israeli rear, the population of which had not been alerted due to the need to surprise the enemy. Israel also avoided sending its people to shelters immediately after the strike as part of denying its responsibility for the raid. If Israel had officially alerted its population, it would have been a kind of admission of guilt.

In 2007, Israel took quite a gamble that paid off since Syria did not retaliate. If there is an Israeli attack on Iranian nuclear sites there is a probability that Iran would immediately retaliate by launching its long-range missiles at Israel. However, Iran has much less capability of hitting Israel than Syria had in 2007, unless the Hezbollah fires its tens of thousands of rockets from Lebanon.

If Israel strikes Iran it would have much more difficulty, compared with 2007, claiming its forces did not bomb Iran, considering the enormous tension between the two states on this issue. This increases the chances of Iranian retribution. But in order to gain surprise Israel might not warn its people in advance to be ready to absorb missiles and rockets.

Once the bombs hit Iran, Israel would put its population in full alert. If Israel attacks at night it could be easier for the Israeli air crews, as well as for Israeli authorities to access the civilian population who would likely be at home and near their shelters there. If the attack occurred during the day, many Israelis would be outside their home, at work, shopping, stuck in traffic, etc. and not necessarily knowing where to find cover if there is an alarm. It could be the same on the weekend and on holidays when many Israelis travel around the country.

For a raid in Iran the IDF could rely on its regulars and a tiny percent of mobilized reserve troops, mostly from the home front command and the IAF, which include the air defense. Police and other public services would be called in too. Those steps should be executed in the last minute as part of keeping the element of surprise. The preparations in the weeks, days, and hours before the attack should be done in secret in camps around the country. Iran does not have measures like satellites to monitor those bases.

Some of IDF preparations for a strike in Iran would be more difficult to hide, such as deployment of anti-aircraft and anti-missile batteries across the country, particularly those that would be positioned near major cities. Soon enough the presence of those units would be an open secret. The national and the local media might be restrained and kept from reporting it, but other media sources would reveal it. Israel would probably have several hours until everyone, including Iran, understood that the IDF was suddenly conducting a massive drill or an actual attack against Iran or the Hezbollah, which could be part of an Israeli offensive against Iran. This is assuming that Iran's Lebanese protégé would be part of its retribution, so Israel has to be ready for a war in Lebanon too.

All that would be clear from the news updates and pictures that would spread around, showing the type of Israeli weapon system that would be in the field. Iron Dome batteries would be deployed in the center and north of Israel, directed against the rockets of the Hezbollah, while Arrow batteries would be used against the kind of missiles that Iran possesses, although the Hezbollah might have some of those missiles too. Israel could avoid deploying in advance many of its anti-aircraft units, not just to maintain the element of surprise, but also based on the assumption that there is a low probability that Iran would send planes to attack Israel and that even if Iran did it, Israeli aircraft could handle them on their own.

Iran could monitor Israel from Lebanon and Syria in order to estimate when an Israeli surprise attack might come.[44] If Iran concludes that an Israeli offensive is imminent, Iran could launch a preemptive strike on Israel against air fields from which Israeli planes would take off. Yet without a smoking gun, i.e., convincing proof for the international community that Israel was indeed about to attack, Iran would appear to be the aggressor. In such a case, even if Iran struck only specific military objectives in Israel, the latter would have a legitimate cause to retaliate and might then bomb Iranian nuclear sites, which are not clear military targets.

On the operational level, Iran could not neutralize the IAF. Even if Iran's missiles carried chemical warheads, it should not prevent the IAF from scrambling planes.

Iran's response to an Israeli attack

An Israeli raid on Iran might cause the people there to feel humiliated and rally around the government. Iranians who experienced the Iraqi invasion in 1980 and still carry that trauma with them might consider Israel's raid another invasion. Many Iranians, including from the opposition, might separate between their loyalty to their country and their criticism of the regime. They could support the government, particularly in acts against Israel. Chances are that no one in Iran would dare to publicly accuse their leadership of provoking Israel to attack.

There are all kinds of scenarios of how a war between Israel and Iran might look.[45] In a war game that was conducted in 2012 at INSS, it was concluded that Iran had limited capability to strike Israel directly, so it would rely on its protégées. There was a need to create a wedge between Iran and its partners in order to avoid escalation. Containing the crisis would have depended on U.S. "clear resolve to stand with Israel and a restrained policy on Israel's part, especially if the strategic objectives of the attack were met in the initial attack." Russia was not considered a credible mediator, but maybe China could have been one.[46]

Hassan Rouhani assumed in late January 2014 that Israel's threats to attack Iran "are empty slogans. When it comes to practice, the Israelis cannot do that. If they do such a crazy thing, our response will make them rue the day."[47] Yet Yossi Kuperwasser, former director general of Israel's Ministry of Strategic Affairs, claimed in June 2015 that following an attack on Iran "the regime would not risk everything if its nuclear program is hit hard, as it knows well how vulnerable Iran is. It might retaliate in a way that saves face, but any such act would be dramatically less painful than the damage that would be caused by Iran acquiring a nuclear bomb."[48]

Iran might retaliate immediately in several ways. One of them would be dispatching SU-24s, long-range attack aircraft, but they don't have the range to reach Israel without air refueling. If they could not land and refuel in Iran's allies, Iraq or Syria, Iran might still send them, knowing they would not have enough fuel to return. However, even if some Iranian SU-24s reached Israel, the IAF (being on high alert at such a time) could intercept them, considering its vast experience and capability in this field.

Iran has hundreds of long-range surface-to-surface missiles that could hit Israel. Iran has been continuing to improve its missiles. During the Second World War, British bombers were not accurate enough to destroy specific targets, so the aim of their bombardments switched to breaking the will of the enemy.[49] Iran's Shahab–3 could hit objectives, but not with the same accuracy as planes. Iran therefore could use its missiles to demoralize the Israeli population by attacking major cities. Iran could also target military camps, airfields, and Israel's nuclear reactor, following Israel's raid on Iranian nuclear sites. Iraq tried to do the same in 1991 as revenge for the destruction of its reactor in 1981.

At least some of the Iranian missiles might be intercepted by Israel's Arrow anti-ballistic missile system. Iran might try to launch many missiles at once in order to overwhelm the Arrow. Iran's launchers might be attacked by Israeli aircraft and maybe by Special Forces too. Yet finding those launchers would be quite a challenge if they were dispersed and hidden in Iran's vast territory.

If Iran manages to pound Israel, the two states might be dragged into a war of attrition, including an exchange of punches on civilian targets as happened between Iran and Iraq during their bitter showdown in the 1980s. Both sides, perhaps particularly Israel, might not wish to continue this clash for an extended period of time. Israel might call for a ceasefire, but if Iran refused or raised too many demands for accepting that, Israel might escalate the war in order to push Iran to end the mutual strikes.

Iran might absorb the Israeli strike on its nuclear sites without retaliating if it reckoned that doing so would not serve its interests. Iran might conclude that it was better not to become entangled in a war for several reasons, primarily urgent affairs such as its economy and the war in Iraq and Syria. Knowing that Israel would be ready for a fierce Iranian retribution may also play a part.

Iran's incentive may be moderated if just light damage was caused to its nuclear infrastructure. An Iranian retribution, particularly against Israeli cities, would give Israel legitimacy to attack Iran again. Iran has limited capability to hit Israel and could depend on its proxies like the Hezbollah, which might disappoint Iran and not join it. Furthermore, by showing restraint, Iran could emphasize to the international community that it was the victim, which might help free the country from sanctions. On the other hand, Iran might look weak to both Arabs and Iranians. Still, Iran might conclude that sometimes revenge is a dish best served cold. For Iran, being in an ongoing Cold War with Israel since the early 1980s, a shooting war could wait for a better opportunity. Meanwhile Iran might launch terror attacks worldwide without taking responsibility for them. Iran also could use its cyber capability, which has improved in recent years.

The capture of the ship Klos-C by Israel: Striking far with Arab help

On March 10, 2014, Israel showed the world the weapons and ammunitions that were seized on the Klos-C, a ship that was captured by Israel 5 days before. The vessel had on it various weapons, including forty M-302 missiles. If they had reached their probable destination, the Gaza Strip, the IDF might not have managed to destroy those missiles before they were launched and the Iron Dome might not have been able to intercept those projectiles.

The operation was conducted by Israel's navy and intelligence community as part of Israel's "campaign between the wars." This is what the IDF calls a prolonged struggle, aimed mostly at reducing as much as possible the transferring of weapons to Iran's protégés and allies in Lebanon and the Gaza Strip.

In the Red Sea, where the Klos-C was seized, several Arab states could have opposed Israeli military activity there. Saudi Arabia, with hundreds of kilometers of shoreline, considers Iran a sworn foe and fears Iran's nuclear project. Saudi Arabia might hope that Israel would attack Iran's nuclear sites, particularly since the United States is not demonstrating any intention of doing that. As a result, Saudi Arabia does not want Iran to supply its protégés in the Gaza Strip with missiles to make Israel think twice before attacking Iran.

Israel's military vessels could sail from the Mediterranean Sea to the Red Sea the short way, through Egypt, i.e., the Suez Canal, as it was done in capturing the Klos-C. The much longer way is to bypass all of Africa, which the Israeli navy did in the past on several occasions. Egypt needs to make it easier for Israel to stop the smuggling of Iranian weapons into Egyptian land, i.e., the Sinai, on their way to the Gaza Strip. Both Egypt and Israel wish to prevent the smuggling of weapons into Sinai by intercepting them in the Red Sea, as part of reducing the influence of Iran.

Israel has been preparing to strike Iranian nuclear sites, located more than a thousand kilometers from Israel. It would be a long-range operation, immeasurably more dangerous than the one on the Klos-C. Such an Israeli raid would require the help, albeit clearly unofficial, of Arab states like Saudi Arabia, over which Israeli aircraft might pass. There could be all kinds of understandings and collaborations, including military ones, between Israel and the Arabs against Iran.

Notes

1 Samuel Segev, *The Iranian Triangle* (Jerusalem, Israel: Domino Press, 1989), 29-110.

2 Abner Yaniv, *Politics and Strategy in Israel* (Tel Aviv: Sifriat Poalim, 1994), 291.

3 On the secret war between Israel and Iran see: Yoaz Hendel, and Yaakov Katz, *Israel vs. Iran: The Shadow War* (Dulles: Virginia Potomac Books, 2012). Ephraim Kam, *From Terror to Nuclear Bombs: The Significance of the Iranian Threat*, (Tel Aviv: Ministry of Defense, 2004). Ronen Bergman, *Point of No Return* (Or Yehuda: Kinneret, Zmora–Bitan, Dvir, 2007). Josef Olmert, "Israel and the Middle East after the Arab Spring: Challenges and Opportunities," in *The Middle East: New Order or Disorder?*, eds. Mohammed A. Aman, and Mary Jo Aman MLIS (Westphalia Press, 2016), 185.

4 Suzanne Maloney, "Oops, He Did It Again: Iran's Supreme Leader Questions the Holocaust," *Brookings*, March 22, 2014, http://www.brookings.edu/blogs/iran-at-saban/posts/2014/03/22-khamenei-holocaust-denial-new-year-speech.

5 John W. Limbert, *Negotiating with Iran* (Washington, DC: United States Institute of Peace, 2009), 19.

6 Kenneth M. Pollack, *Unthinkable: Iran, the Bomb, and American Strategy* (New York: Simon & Schuster, 2013), 11.

7 The Washington Post, May 1, 2015, http://www.washingtonpost.com/blogs/fact-checker/wp/2015/05/01/irans-claim-that-israel-has-400-nuclear-weapons/.

8 Jerusalem Post, February 24, 2016, http://www.jpost.com/Opinion/Shaping-Israels-military-nuclear-doctrine-446003.

9 Avi Primor, "No Permanent Allies, No Permanent Enemies, Only Permanent Interests": Israeli–Iranian Relations," *Israel Journal of Foreign Affairs* 8 (1) (January 2014): 37.

10 Jeffrey Herf, "Taking Iran's Anti-Semitism Seriously," *The American Interest*, June 2, 2014, http://www.the-american-interest.com/2014/06/02/taking-irans-anti-semitism-seriously/.

11 Charles D. Freilich, *Zion's Dilemmas—How Israel Makes National Security Policy* (Cornell University Press, 2012).

12 Defense One, May 20, 2014, http://www.defenseone.com/ideas/2014/05/leave-ballistic-missiles-out-iran-nuclear-talks/84778/.

13 Matthew Kroenig, *A Time to Attack* (New York: Palgrave Macmillan, 2014), 31.

14 Haaretz, March 19, 2014, http://www.haaretz.com/news/diplomacy-defense/1.580701.

15 BesaCenter, April24, 2014, http://besacenter.org/perspectives-papers/israel-accept-emerging-according-us-iran/.

16 Ynet, May 29, 2014, http://www.ynet.co.il/articles/0,7340,L-4525241,00.html. See also Alarabiya, November 28, 2013, http://english.alarabiya.net/en/perspective/analysis/2013/11/28/Israel-struggling-to-win-friends-influence-people.html.

17 The Council on Foreign Relations (CFR), Preventive Priorities Survey: 2015, December 2014, http://www.cfr.org/peace-conflict-and-human-rights/preventive-priorities-survey-2015/p33990.

18 The Times of Israel, February 12, 2015, http://www.timesofisrael.com/minister-warns-of-potential-action-against-iran/.

19 The Times of Israel, March 15, 2015, http://www.timesofisrael.com/zionist-unions-soft-spoken-nuclear-bombardier/.

20 Besa Center, March 19, 2015, http://besacenter.org/uncategorized/security-challenges-of-the-new-israeli-government/.

21 Institute for National Security Studies (INSS), May 18, 2014, http://www.inss.org.il/index.aspx?id=4538&articleid=6993.

22 Nrg, June 16, 2015, http://www.nrg.co.il/online/1/ART2/702/451.html?hp=1&cat=875.

23 The Times of Israel, June 25, 2015, http://www.timesofisrael.com/air-force-key-to-defending-against-iran-netanyahu-says/.

24 The Times of Israel, July 14, 2015, http://www.timesofisrael.com/barak-iran-likely-to-become-nuclear-within-decade/.

25 Algemeiner, October 1, 2015, http://www.algemeiner.com/2015/10/01/full-transcript-prime-minister-netanyahus-speech-at-the-united-nations-general-assembly-2015-video/.

26 Defense News, January 7, 2016, http://www.defensenews.com/story/defense/policy-budget/policy/2016/01/07/israels-5-year-plan-bulks-up-combat-capabilities-cuts-manpower/78421050/.

27 The Iran Primer, http://iranprimer.usip.org/resource/military-option.

28 On 1967 see: Ailn Cfir, and Yakob Arz, eds., *The IDF in His Core—The Artillery* (Tel Aviv: Rbibim, 1982), 110.

29 On Amos Yadlin see: the New Republic, October 23, 2013, http://www.newrepublic.com/article/115313/amos-yadlin-iran-strike-why-israel-needs-act-soon.

30 Steven R. David, *Fatal Choices: Israel's Policy of Targeted Killing* (Besa Center, 2002(, 7–11. Naomi Chazan, "Assassinations as Weapons of War," *The Israel Journal of Foreign Affairs* 2 (2) (2008): 85–89.

31 The Free Beacon, August 7, 2012, http://freebeacon.com/national-security/october-surprise/.

32 The New York Times, February 20, 2012, http://www.nytimes.com/2012/02/20/world/middleeast/iran-raid-seen-as-complex-task-for-israeli-military.html?pagewanted=all.

33 CNN, March 13, 2012, http://www.cnn.com/2012/03/13/world/meast/israel-iran-attack/index.html.

34 Epraim Karsh, *The Iran–Iraq War 1980–1988* (Wellingborough, Northants, UK: Osprey, 2002), 17.

35 On Iran's air force: The Washington Institute, May 27, 2016, http://www.washingtoninstitute.org/policy-analysis/view/irans-air-force-overshadowed-by-the-irgc.

36 The Iran Project, September 14, 2015, http://theiranproject.com/blog/2015/09/14/iran-putting-into-service-new-long-range-radar-system/.

37 The Washington Institute for Near East Policy, April 13, 2016, http://www.washingtoninstitute.org/policy-analysis/view/russian-s-300-deliveries-to-iran-have-apparently-begun.

38 The Times of Israel, May 21, 2015, http://www.timesofisrael.com/iran-to-un-israeli-defense-minister-threatened-to-nuke-us/.

39 Center for Strategic International Studies (CSIS), October 27, 2011, http://csis.org/files/publication/111027_Iran_Gulf_Military_Balance.pdf.

40 Reuters, July 3, 2009, http://www.reuters.com/article/2009/07/03/us-israel-iran-submarine-idUSTRE5621XZ20090703. See also: David

Schenker, "Egypt's Enduring Challenges," The Washington Institute for Near East Policy (Policy focus # 110, April 2011), p.25.

41 Yair Evron, "An Israel–Iran Balance of Nuclear Deterrence: Seeds of Instability," in *Israel and a Nuclear Iran: Implications for Arms Control, Deterrence and Defense*, ed. Ephraim Kam (INSS, 2008), 52. David Rodman, "'If I am not for Myself ...' Methods and Motives behind Israel's Quest for Military Self–Reliance," *The Israel Journal of Foreign Affairs* 4 (1) (2010): 58.

42 On the rule of Israeli Special forces see: Whitney Raas, and Austin Long, "Osirak Redux?," *International Security* 31 (4) (Spring 2007): 17.

43 The National Interest, 30 January 2014, http://nationalinterest.org/commentary/bombing-iran-tough-tasks-israeli-intelligence-9789?page=1.

44 The National Interest, April 16, 2014, http://nationalinterest.org/commentary/surprise-attack-iran-can-israel-do-it-10253?page=4.

45 See for example: http://www.biu.ac.il/SOC/besa/MSPS82.pdf.

46 Udi Dekel, and Yonathan Lerner, "War Game: The Hours Following an Attack on Iran's Nuclear Infrastructures—The Policies of the Actors and Principal Insights," *INSS Insight* (No. 382, November four, 2012), http://www.inss.org.il/index.aspx?id=4538&articleid=5195.

47 The Hill, January 24, 2014, http://thehill.com/blogs/defcon-hill/operations/196358-rouhani-israel-will-not-attack-iran.

48 Yossi Kuperwasser, Israel's Role in the Struggle Over the Iranian Nuclear Project, Besa center, Mideast Security and Policy Studies (No. 114, June 2015), p.25.

49 B. H. Liddell Hart, *History of the Second World War* (London: Book Club Associates, 1970), 595.

Chapter 2

Israel against the Hezbollah

Israel fought the Hezbollah in Lebanon in the 1980s and 1990s, withdrawing from Lebanon in May 2000. In July and August 2006, Israel and the Hezbollah collided again, this time for 34 days. Both sides have been preparing for a future clash ever since. The Hezbollah, a hybrid force and an Iranian proxy, would probably confront Israel if the latter attacked Iran's nuclear sites.

The Iranian nuclear program is a top concern for Israel and a major issue for many states, like western ones that are worried Israel might bomb Iran. Therefore, it is important to understand the possible challenges, hardships, and readiness of Israel for a war against the Hezbollah, as that would influence Israel's decision about if and when to attack Iran.

The struggle between Israel and the Hezbollah

Before 1982, Israel worried that the Palestine Liberation Organization (PLO) in Lebanon was becoming a threat.[1] In 1982, Israel defeated the PLO and forced most of its men to leave Lebanon. Nevertheless, the Israel Defense Forces (IDF) remained in Lebanon and continued to fight there.

In 1985, Israel retreated from most of the area it had conquered in Lebanon, without leaving behind a force powerful and capable enough to prevent attacks against Israel. The latter did create a militia of local Arabs, but this group was unable to hold its ground without IDF deployment near them. Their common enemy was the Hezbollah, which emerged following the Israeli invasion in 1982.[2]

In 2006, there was a war between Israel and the Hezbollah in Lebanon. Since then there have been some minor incidents on the border between Israel and Lebanon that could have deteriorated into a bigger clash between Israel and the Hezbollah, against the will of one or both sides. There have also been assaults by both sides in other places, such as the assassination of Imad Fayez Mughniyeh, one of the most senior figures in the Hezbollah, who was killed in Syria on February 12, 2008, and the murder of five Israeli civilians in Burgas, Bulgaria, on July 18, 2012. In 1982, Israel started a war against the PLO in Lebanon following an assassination attempt on the Israeli ambassador to London by a Palestinian terror group. Yet in July 2012, Israel, just like the Hezbollah in February 2008, did not wish to exploit an assault against itself as a pretext for war. None of those events was a sufficient cause, and neither side wanted to start a confrontation. Those assaults were part of the big cold war between Israel and Iran and the small cold war between Israel and the Iranian proxy, the Hezbollah.

Hezbollah "is founded, trained, supplied, supported, and directed by Iran, and the Hezbollah also has ideological ties to Tehran."[3] The "Lebanese Shi'ites were the most receptive of all Shi'ites to Iran's Islamic revolutionary message."[4] Iran supported the Hezbollah more than it did Iraqi Shi'ite insurgents. This approach had "much to do with the different internal dynamics within these proxy organizations, and their ability to attract and use capabilities provided."[5]

Because of Iran, since 2000 and mostly after the 2006 war, the Hezbollah became more and more of a threat to Israel, mostly due to its huge stockpile of rockets. The IDF could invade Lebanon and inflict a very substantial blow to the Hezbollah, but this could cost Israel dearly in blood and treasure. Furthermore, the Hezbollah might recover or be replaced by other radical groups like Islamic State of Iraq and Syria (ISIS) or those associated with Al Qaeda that could be less rational than the Hezbollah. Another possible outcome might be a clash between the Hezbollah and other

Lebanese groups as well as with Israel. The latter could try creating or supporting a local friendly militia in Lebanon, but this could take months if not years, and there is no guarantee that a new pro-Israel group would manage to hold its ground alone. Israel would probably strongly oppose being pinned down with its forces in Lebanon as during the period from 1982 to 2000.

The Hezbollah supported the Palestinians in their 2000–2005 confrontation with Israel by delivering weapons, money, information how to build improvised explosive devices (IEDs), etc.[6] Yet in the same period, until the 2006 war, it was relatively quiet on the border between Israel and Lebanon, apart from some incidents, the most serious of which occurred in April 2002. All the assaults against Israel from Lebanon in 2000–2006, including the provocation that ignited the war in 2006, did not by themselves require a massive Israeli offensive inside Lebanon. Either way, after 2006 there was almost complete calm on the Israeli–Lebanese border. The two sworn enemies managed to tolerate each other's presence.

In 2003, following the conquest of Iraq, Iran suggested to the United States a comprehensive proposal for negotiations. It included an end to Iranian aid to the Hamas and Islamic Jihad and Iranian support for the disbanding of the Hezbollah, restricting it to being just a political party. Iran had quite a lot of demands as well. The United States refused to start talks. Trita Parsi, the president of the National Iranian American Council, claimed that this opportunity was "willfully wasted."[7] For Iran, however, the talks might have been just a way to buy time and avoid an American attack. The Iranian openness to talks also implied the country's willingness to abandon, temporarily or not, Israel's main foes in the Palestinian camp, the Hamas and Islamic Jihad, and to end the danger to Israel from the Hezbollah.

Iran's Palestinian allies in the Gaza Strip are important to the country since they provide their patron with a bridgehead in the Mediterranean Sea. Yet, the Hezbollah gives Iran a better access to the Mediterranean Sea since Lebanon has harbors that are enormously better and bigger than the one in Gaza, in Beirut, for example. Also, there is an international airport in the Lebanese capital city while the one in the Gaza Strip is out of action.

Israel had difficulty stopping the delivery of Iranian supplies to the Hezbollah in Lebanon, which has a border with Syria, enabling the Hezbollah and Syria to cooperate and assist each other. The Hamas in the Gaza Strip, on the other hand, is stuck between two rivals of Iran, Israel, and Egypt. Iran did manage to smuggle weapons, manpower, etc. to the Gaza Strip through the Sinai, an Egyptian territory. For Iran, the peninsula is the end of a long and problematic line of communication, while the one that goes to the Hezbollah is shorter, particularly when the supplies come directly from Assad. Another advantage of the Hezbollah, as far as Iran is concerned, is that its fighters are Shi'ites, while the Hamas are Sunnis. All those differences explain the huge Iranian investment in the Hezbollah.

Would the Hezbollah join Iran in a war against Israel?

Sami Nader, the Director of the Levant Institute for Strategic Affairs, said in late July 2016 that "Hezbollah may be tempted to engage Israel in what it hopes is a limited war to recover their prestige."[8] The Hezbollah could, therefore, seek a confrontation with Israel in order to boost its popularity in Lebanon. Furthermore, if Israel attacked Iran, the latter's retribution would rely on the Hezbollah. In another scenario, if Israel gets entangled in the fight inside Syria against Iran's allies such as Assad, Iran might order the Hezbollah to strike Israel, although in past cases involving Hezbollah's partners attacked by Israel, Iran did not react. In 2007, Israel destroyed the Syrian nuclear reactor, thereby denying a main ally of the Hezbollah a game-changing weapon. In 2008–2009, Israel struck the Hamas in the Gaza Strip, a partner of Iran and the Hezbollah, with no consequences.

The Hezbollah has been kept as an Iranian fire base to be used at Iran's pleasure. Iranian officers from the Islamic Revolutionary Guard Corps (IRGC) have been operating closely with the leader of the Hezbollah, Hassan Nasrallah, and the group's top brass in order to make sure that the Hezbollah follows Iranian commands.[9] Iran has, therefore, quite a grip on the Hezbollah, including its decision making,[10] but in spite of the ties to Iran, the Hezbollah might think twice before confronting Israel. The IDF is much more powerful than the Hezbollah and could hit it hard, attempting to annihilate this group. Nasrallah believes in sacrifice as a tactical measure. He would send his men to dangerous and even suicidal missions but would avoid the destruction of the organization itself.

During the years since 2000, if there had been a war between Israel and the Hezbollah, Iran could have sent the Hezbollah supplies and maybe even some troops through Iraq and Syria, albeit on a limited scale. Dispatching tens of thousands of Iranian troops would have been a tall order for Iran. Its troops would have had to pass hundreds of kilometers, partly in Iraqi territory, which would have been quite problematic, to put it mildly, while Saddam Hussein was still in power. Israel was Hussein's enemy, but his relations with Iran were shaky and full of mutual suspicion. Allowing tens of thousands of well-armed Iranians to cross Iraq might have seemed to Saddam Hussein like a trick aimed at striking him, with the help of Iraqi Shi'ites and Kurds.

Since 2003 during the American deployment in Iraq, there has obviously been no option of dispatching thousands of Iranian troops through Iraq. Even in recent years, in spite of the close cooperation between the Iraqi government and Iran, including supporting Assad, allowing an Iranian expeditionary force into Iraq would not have been that simple. Iraq might have been concerned about drawing too much international criticism and would have been worried about the response of Iraqi Sunnis, Kurds, and Gulf Arab states.

Israel, whose air force trains to bomb targets farther than Iraq, might have struck not only Iranian columns on Iraqi soil but also Iraqi objectives, as retribution for allowing the Iranian military to cross that country on its way to fight Israel. Iraq would have been helplessly exposed to bombardments since it has no modern air defense or air force.

Iran would have had enormous logistical and operational constraints in deploying several divisions more than a thousand kilometers from their bases. This is a major challenge even for a highly organized and trained military, and the Iranian armed forces are not very effective, with no experience in conducting such a move. The Iranian regime would have also hesitated to dispatch its best troops, particularly the revolutionary guards, so far away from home. Such a move might have encouraged Iranian citizens opposed to the military adventure in Lebanon and/or the regime itself to create unrest within their country.

Furthermore, Iran might have ended up carrying the main burden of the fighting on the frontline. Having never excelled at high-intensity war, the Iranian military would have faced the might of the IDF, which would have had the additional advantage of being close to its home base. The IDF would have inflicted on Iran's expeditionary force a humiliating defeat, which might have undermined the rule in Iran. Israel might have also exploited the Iranian intervention in Lebanon as a pretext to attack Iran's nuclear sites. For those reasons it would be very unlikely that Iran would send large forces to Lebanon in a future war between Israel and the Hezbollah.

During the 2006 war, the Assad regime, the Hezbollah's most vital Arab ally, did not intervene. If in 2006-2011 there had been another round between Israel and the Hezbollah, the latter would have needed Assad more than it did in 2006. Since 2011, due to the civil war in Syria, the Hezbollah could not have relied on Assad. The latter has been too weak to start a second front from Syria against Israel or to send major reinforcements. This is another reason for the Hezbollah to avoid challenging Israel.

The Hezbollah is worn down from the fights in Syria. If this process continues, it might encourage Israel to attack the Hezbollah, as part of a raid on Iran or not, assuming the Hezbollah is vulnerable. Hezbollah troops, who were supposed to defend their rockets from attacks by Israeli ground units, would numerically and morally erode because of the battles in Syria.

For the Hezbollah getting entangled in the war in Syria might be much less destructive than confronting Israel. The Israeli attacks would be much more powerful than those of Syrian Sunni rebels furious as they were at the Hezbollah for its military intervention in their country.

Israel might attack Iran and the Hezbollah simultaneously. Militarily it is much easier for Israel to attack Hezbollah than to strike Iran, due to the proximity of the Hezbollah to Israel. An offensive against the Hezbollah depends on Israel's estimate of if, when and to what extent the Hezbollah would confront Israel. It remains to be seen which party retaliates more harshly, the Lebanese organization or Iran.

If the Hezbollah and not Iran counterattacks Israel, or at least does most of the fighting, and fires a barrage of missiles at the civilian population, the Hezbollah will have to face most of the Israeli backlash. The cost of war for the Hezbollah might be enormous, but Iran, which expects its own people to take a risk, would no doubt accept that the Hezbollah might pay a high price, since it serves as Iran's fire base and bulletproof vest. Also, Iran is mostly Shi'ite and mostly Persian, while the Hezbollah is Shi'ite but Arab, not Persian or Iranian. This fact is probably well considered by the Hezbollah.

If there is a war between Israel and Iran, the latter could pay a high price, not the least of it a destroyed economy. The Iranian leaders might decide that in order to survive they must concentrate on internal affairs. In the past, the Iranian regime made tough decisions that it did not like: ending the war with Iraq in 1988, freezing Iran's nuclear program in 2003, etc. Nothing is more valuable to the Iranian leadership than its survival. Hezbollah is important to

Iran and gives it a hold in Lebanon, but the latter is one of the smallest and weakest Arab countries. Lebanon does not have a major strategic value compared with other Arab countries like Syria, with its size and location, or the oil in Iraq and Arab states in the Gulf and the Suez Canal in Egypt.

It is possible that after a war in which Israel performs a successful defense against both Iran and the Hezbollah in Lebanon, Iran might assume it had underestimated Israel's power. This may not convince Iran to soften its approach toward Israel; rather, it may lead Iran to reevaluate the Hezbollah's arsenal, estimating it was insufficient to deter Israel. However, if Iran rearmed the Hezbollah, would this make much of a difference? In the past Israel attacked Arab militaries that were stronger than the Hezbollah would ever be.

After a war with Israel, Iran might reconsider the extent of its influence in the Levant, specifically in Lebanon. A shift, temporary or not, in Iran's strategy could reduce the transfer of funds from Iran to the Hezbollah. This would impact the rebuilding of both the Hezbollah and the civilian infrastructure of its supporters. The funds for those purposes that Iran allocated after the 2006 war were essential for the recovery of the Hezbollah.

Following another war in Lebanon, the Hezbollah might require even more aid than in 2006 to restore its military and political power. This need is based on the fact that Hezbollah is entrenched inside villages. During a war those places would be exposed to major destruction due to massive use of Israeli firepower. If Hezbollah had no large amounts of money to rebuild and compensate the civilians, it would lose local support and run into trouble.

The Hezbollah has established in Lebanon a kind of state within a state. The group holds a dominant position in Lebanon, which took many years to form with the help of its Lebanese allies. The Hezbollah might find itself in a weak spot after a war against Israel, which would be an opportunity for its rivals in Lebanon, particularly if the war caused extensive damage to that country.

There might be a strong public demand in Lebanon to disarm the Hezbollah, whose weapons are one of the foundations of its political power. A war against Israel, therefore, might jeopardize the influence of both Hezbollah and its Lebanese partners. Iran, having a prolonged investment in that country, might not wish to risk undermining the grip it has on Lebanon through its protégé.

The Hezbollah has been a sworn enemy of Israel since the 1980s, but as with Iran, there is no real territorial dispute between them, at least nothing like the one between Israel and the Palestinians.

Before the Israeli withdrawal in 2000, the Hezbollah was aware that its military activity might end when Israel left Lebanon.[11] Daniel Byman, research director of the Saban Center for Middle East Policy, mentioned Israel's hope that the Hezbollah would turn into a "more normal, less violent political movement."[12] This did not happen. Moreover, since Israel's withdrawal from Lebanon, the Hezbollah has been demanding that Israel hand over the Shebaa farms to Lebanon. This is an area of about 10 square kilometers on the border between Israel and Lebanon, mostly empty and without any substantial value, but it served as an excuse for Hezbollah to hold on to its weapons. For Israel the area is necessary to access vital posts on Mount Harmon.

Israel would have agreed to relinquish the Shebaa farms to Syria as part of a peace treaty or transfer the territory to the government of Lebanon but not to the Hezbollah. The latter has been also demanding an Israeli withdrawal from an area of seven Shi'ite villages abandoned in the 1948-49 war, spread across most of the Israeli border with Lebanon. Obviously Israel refuses this demand. The UN, not exactly a pro-Israel organization, confirmed in 2000 the current location of the border between Israel and Lebanon as the official one.

Hezbollah's territorial demands and rejection of Israel's right to exist, along with its dreams of marching to Jerusalem, are part of its propaganda war. Getting back the Shebaa farms and the seven villages from the 1948-49 war are not that significant for Lebanon, let alone the Arab world. Wiping out Israel, another Hezbollah goal, is obviously something this organization could never accomplish alone. Bigger and more important Arab players than the Lebanese group have accepted that Israel is here to stay, following peace treaties with Israel or showing their willingness to sign such an accord with it.

Changing the Hezbollah's rhetoric might be quite easy, particularly for a skillful speaker like Nasrallah, who seems able to talk his way out of many complicated situations. Instead of risking an entanglement in a dangerous showdown with Israel, he could focus on strengthening his position in Lebanon. It might be an essential move for the Hezbollah, especially if its Sunni rivals, such as those in Syria, increase their attacks against the Hezbollah in Lebanon. Israel might continue tolerating the Hezbollah, its survival and even its rule in Lebanon, if it refrains from attacking the Jewish state. Israel has already been carrying out this policy with other Arab rulers.

In January 2016 IDF Chief of General Staff Lt. Gen. Gadi Eizenkot emphasized that the Hezbollah is Israel's "central threat."[13] IDF Intelligence Chief Major General Herzl Halevi argued on June 15, 2016, that in the next war "Hezbollah will lose its political support base." Regarding Israeli intelligence on the Hezbollah, Halevi said, "I say with all due caution that I think that never before has an army known as much about its enemy as we know about Hezbollah."[14]

All in all, for all kinds of reasons—mostly fear of absorbing a heavy blow—the Hezbollah might restrain itself during a war between Iran and Israel, demonstrating its solidarity with its Iranian patron by randomly firing a few of its rockets, maybe even aiming at open fields, hoping that Israel would do the same in Lebanon. Israel, while fighting Iran, might not wish to open a second front up north and could avoid attacking in Lebanon if casualties and damages on its side were minor. Iran too might order its protégé to keep a low profile until Iran gets nuclear weapons. In spite of all these considerations, the Hezbollah, with strong Iranian encouragement, might open fire on a massive scale, intending to harm Israel with everything it has.

Arab policy during a war between Israel and the Hezbollah

The Hezbollah, as a Shi'ite organization, would receive hardly any sympathy from Arab states with Sunni majorities. Those states like Saudi Arabia would probably support, unofficially, an Israeli attack on the Hezbollah. They would like to see a reduction and if possible the end of the grip the Shi'ite organization has on Lebanon, clearing the way for the Sunnis there to seize control.

In the 1982 war, Israel was burned by its collaboration with the Christians of Lebanon against the PLO. Still a massive penetration of the IDF into Lebanon in the future might convince the Hezbollah's rivals to collaborate with the IDF by delivering information about the Hezbollah's strength and the location of its rockets. This might be done secretly since the Hezbollah's foes do not support Israel and do not want to be seen as such. They would strive to weaken the Hezbollah and to end the war quickly, thus limiting the damage to their country.

The PA is not an ally of Iran or the Hezbollah, and there is a rift between Iran and the Hamas following the war in Syria. There might be a simultaneous confrontation between Israel and the Palestinians in the West Bank and/or the Gaza Strip while Israel collides with the Hezbollah, without a direct connection between those confrontations. The IDF's options would be staying in the West Bank/Gaza Strip in a defensive position until the war in Lebanon was over and then going on the offensive against the Palestinians, or not waiting that long. The IDF does not need more than a few divisions on the two Palestinian fronts, due to the relative weakness of its foes and the nature of the combat there.

Israel's aim: destroying the rockets

The mutual tension between Israel and the Hezbollah exploded in the 2006 war, although it was not clear exactly what Israel's goals were then.[15] Israel failed to reach a decision. It seems that Israel's offensive was not an all-out effort to destroy the Hezbollah but more a major attempt to punish and restrain it. Israel's declarations reflected more of a wish than a serious intention to crush the Hezbollah.

There is an asymmetry between Israel and the Hezbollah due to the military might of the former. The Hezbollah could only dream of destroying the IDF and conquering Israel. The latter could seize all the area the Hezbollah occupies in Lebanon but not necessarily wipe it out since this nonstate organization would continue to fight from the underground.

A full-scale attack deep into Lebanon might lead, as it did in 1982, to hundreds of casualties among Israeli troops, severe disputes inside Israel and other negative ramifications after sinking into a quagmire inside Lebanon.[16] The grim memory from 1982 was not necessarily overshadowed by the 2006 war. Thus, in the next war Israel would probably be determined to avoid the mistakes and the certain humiliation of the 2006 war while avoiding a long and frustrating deployment in Lebanon. The IDF would strive to achieve its goals quickly and then withdraw from Lebanon. The IDF's aims would be limited, mostly to stop or at least to limit as much as possible the firing of rockets from Lebanon.

The fire base the PLO had built in Lebanon, threatening mostly the north of Israel, was annihilated in 1982. Although this Palestinian stronghold was gradually replaced by Hezbollah rockets, it took the latter many years to match the capability the PLO had in 1982. A very small number of rockets hit the north of Israel ten years later, in 1992.[17] During a major Israeli operation in Lebanon in April 1996, the Hezbollah fired about 500 rockets into the north of Israel.[18] In comparison in mid-July 1981 the PLO launched about

1,200 rockets and shells into Israel. It is probable that only after the year 2000 and perhaps after the 2006 war the Hezbollah obtained the firepower the PLO had in the early 1980s. The Hezbollah relies on rockets while the PLO also had artillery pieces like guns.

The Hezbollah had about 10,000 rockets in 2003,[19] 30,000 rockets in 2006[20] and up to 70,000 rockets in 2013,[21] and in 2016 the Hezbollah has 150,000 rockets. [22] This huge increase might have happened anyway, but the 2006 war encouraged Iran and the Hezbollah to accelerate the delivery of rockets to Lebanon. The growing arsenal of the Hezbollah might push Israel to attack it before it becomes more dangerous. Israel could therefore launch an offensive against the Hezbollah without striking Iran's nuclear sites.

Yet a preventive war against the Hezbollah might be difficult to explain not only to the international community but inside Israel as well. Considering the possible high price of such a war for Israel, it is essential to convince the population that there was a solid argument for waging war against the Hezbollah. After all, as long as the latter does not fire on Israel, the situation could be tolerated. In this sense the Hezbollah would be like other Arab militaries such as the Syrian one, which had several divisions near the Israeli border in the Golan Heights for many years. Those Syrian units could have stormed the border on short notice, but Israel never tried to prevent that danger by initiating a war.

"For Israel, the paradox is that, although in the long term, it would appreciate the fall of Hezbollah, in the short term, it may prefer a strong Hezbollah that maintains its hold on south Lebanon and its control over its arsenal."[23] If the Hezbollah crumbled, Israel would be worried that all kinds of groups of Islamic extremists might seize the rockets or some of them. For Israel the Hezbollah is the devil you know, easier to deter than other radical groups.

On June 14, 2016, Major-General (res.) Yitzhak Gershon, who commands the IDF's reservist northern region emergency division, said that while in the war of 2006, 160 rockets were fired every day, in the next war up to 1,200 rockets could be fired in a day.[24] The Hezbollah might focus on sensitive targets like industry or airfields or on a certain city. The Hezbollah might inflict more damage on an Israeli city than any other Arab force has done since 1948.

The Hezbollah has several thousand 220 millimeter and 302 millimeter rockets, with a range of up to 150 kilometers, and also the M-600, which could hit targets up to 300 kilometers away quite accurately.[25] Hezbollah's firepower covers all the population centers in Israel. In March 2013 the Hezbollah claimed that "its arsenal has been unaffected by the Syrian turmoil and that it is now capable of paralyzing Israel with long-range rocket strikes, if war erupts."[26] This declaration may cause the IDF to aim at destroying Hezbollah's rockets, especially the long-range ones,[27] before they are launched, as the IDF did in the beginning of the 2006 war.

The Hezbollah could prepare for an Israeli strike on its long-range rockets by hiding them in shelters. Such measures would force Israel to gather accurate intelligence on the location of the rockets, drop bombs powerful enough to penetrate bunkers where rockets were hidden and consider launching a surprise and massive offensive before the rockets were removed. This approach goes back to the first day of the 1967 war, when the IAF annihilated Egyptian long-range bombers on the ground. As in 2006 the Israeli goal in 1967 was to remove the threat to its civilian and military infrastructure in the rear as soon as possible. For the same reason, the IAF might bomb Iranian launchers of long-range missiles during a raid on Iran's nuclear sites.

Hezbollah's rockets are deployed in about 200 villages and towns in Lebanon, in "garages, basements, barns, bedrooms, and tunnels."[28] The location of some of Hezbollah's rockets is known to the IDF from aerial photos. Other rockets could be exposed during the war if the IDF fired on a suspected area in order to bring the Hezbollah's position to reveal itself.[29] Some of the IDF's intelligence units that are trained in discovering targets would make observations in the field. Israel's intelligence community has plenty on its plate since it gathers information on other foes mostly in Iran, Syria, the Gaza Strip, the West Bank, and Sinai.

The Hezbollah could try to jam GPS and by that to divert some of Israel's guided missiles. They might miss their targets and harm the population by mistake.[30] The Hezbollah may attempt to escape a bombardment by deploying mobile rocket launchers, but they would be exposed when they were on the move, including at night. The IDF could also be hindered by harsh weather. However, its experience bombing rockets in the Gaza Strip could assist in Lebanon as there too the rockets are inside urban areas.

In past wars the IDF sometimes assimilated, even immediately, captured weapons that were in turn used against the enemy. Although the IDF could seize some of the Hezbollah rockets, Israel would not fire them into Lebanon, since most of them are inaccurate and might cause collateral damage. Israel could transfer the rockets to UN units in Lebanon or to anti-Hezbollah forces in Lebanon, but they would not be trusted. The IDF would probably prefer to transfer them to Israel, as was done in the 1982 war in Lebanon, when the IDF loaded hundreds of trucks with weapons that were taken as spoils of war. The IDF could also blow up all the rockets that would be found together with the infrastructure that hid them.

The IDF could gather material from Hezbollah's strongholds like documents, computers with data, etc., after which the IDF would abandon the site, unless that spot was essential for further operations or controlled a key route. If that were not the case, the Israeli force would move on to its next objective.

Conquering territory in Lebanon would not be planned, in order to prevent the military and political hardships of occupying Arab land. If Israel remained in Lebanon, it would be easier for the Hezbollah to present it as an invader, to avoid taking responsibility for the war and to silence criticism against the Hezbollah in Lebanon.

The Hezbollah did not gain CW from Syria, an arsenal that could have served it as a last option to deter Israel from penetrating deep into Lebanon and/or assassinating the leadership of the Hezbollah. Already the latter might threaten or actually launch its rockets, carrying explosives, at highly sensitive sites inside Israel, such as the chemical industry in Haifa, which potentially might cause a major disaster in one of the most populated cities in Israel. Such a concern would necessitate the destruction of all Hezbollah rockets able to reach Haifa.

Israeli preparations

Avi Kober, a senior research associate at the Begin-Sadat Center for Strategic Studies, mentioned in 2009 that the IDF tactical doctrine from 1963 has been updated in recent years and its operational concept "crystallized." However, the IDF deals mostly with high-intensity war and "regular" war, not irregular fighters or attrition wars.[31] In 2014 the IDF, as part of its preparations to fight the Hezbollah, developed "battle doctrine based on the need to operate in enemy's depth. It is focused on how to get forces there, how to fight in closed spaces, destroy tunnels, and take on fortified targets."[32] Yet Ephraim Inbar said in February 2015 that "if Israel makes preparations for a large-scale operation against Hezbollah." This means building the necessary ground forces and training for Lebanese scenarios. Such a build-up process is not clearly evident so far."[33] In early May 2015 the IDF's 36th division conducted a large exercise in the Jordan rift valley, aimed against the Hezbollah. On August 13, 2015, the IDF published the "IDF Strategy," which was also aimed against the Hezbollah.[34] In March 2016 the IAF carried out a huge exercise that tested its units during a large-scale rocket attack on Israel.

Maj. Gen. Yair Golan, as the head of the Israeli Northern Command, argued in early May 2014 that the IDF should learn from the 1948-49 war, because it was a showdown where company commanders played a key role, and today the IDF focuses on fighting in small formations.[35] In addition, during the 1982 war in Lebanon, the IDF deployed—for the first time in combat—several of its divisions as part of a corps. In the years that followed, the corps remained, but its status declined since the IDF focused on the struggle against the Palestinians and the Hezbollah, which demanded much smaller formations than a corps. After the 2006 war in Lebanon, the IDF invested again in the corps. It might be needed for high-intensity war against Egypt but less in a clash against the Hezbollah.

The Hezbollah might launch a first strike at Israel. Such a blow might catch the IDF and its reserves unprepared. A more predictable scenario is that a raid on Iran could bring on a war between Israel and the Hezbollah. In a raid on Iran, Israel would rely on the IAF, i.e., on a few thousand troops such as ground and air crews. Many of them are regular or career troops, so the IAF could conduct the air attack without calling in most of its reserves, which would help keep the element of surprise.

In contrast a ground offensive against the Hezbollah would require large-scale mobilization. Tens of thousands of Israeli reserves would leave their homes from all over the country. Such ongoing activity would be hard to hide, and Iran or the Hezbollah might find out about it. The Hezbollah would put its men on alert, particularly if Israeli troops were concentrated near the border with Lebanon and not on other fronts, an obvious fact revealing Israel's goals. This might even lead the Hezbollah to strike first. Iran might go on alert too.

In order to maintain the element of surprise, the IDF would probably wait until its planes dropped the bombs on Iran before calling its reserves for a possible fight in Lebanon. This is based on the assumption that attacking Iran is more important to Israel than striking the Hezbollah. It is also self-evident that keeping secret a massive deployment for an attack against the Hezbollah would be much more difficult than gathering a much smaller force for a raid against Iran.

The Hezbollah could launch its rockets as soon as Israel struck Iran. This means tens of thousands of Israeli reserves might be mobilized under fire. Some of Israel's citizen soldiers would have to leave their families while rockets were hitting their homes. Troops might hesitate in that situation, particularly if rockets fell right near their homes. Rockets might also land on bases where Israeli soldiers checked in to get their weapons, vehicles, etc. The Hezbollah might try to monitor and follow IDF movements inside Israel by listening to communications in order to direct fire on Israeli troops.

As long as Hezbollah's arsenal is based mostly on unguided rockets, they could not accurately hit their targets. They could fire their rockets on large objectives such as major bases and main crossroads, where Israeli forces would travel on their way to Lebanon. Other rockets might hit staging areas, forcing Israeli troops to be ready to absorb those bombardments all the way to the frontline. Shooting thousands of rockets on Israeli troops would inflict casualties and damage. It might undermine morale and disrupt Israeli operations even before its troops penetrated Lebanon.

In 2014 budget cuts reduced the number of exercises that were meant to train Israeli troops for such situations.[36] The IDF did conduct a major exercise in early May 2014. Five hundred vehicles, including tanks and artillery, were transported from the south to the north of Israel. Such a drill, which occurs every few years, took into consideration enemy fire on main crossroads. The IDF assumes it might have to bypass crossroads that would be jammed. Also route 6, the Trans-Israeli highway, might be divided during a war. In one direction there would be only military movements. In the other direction, civilians could escape the frontline.[37]

The IDF should gather its reserves in safe places and protect assembly areas. Indeed in those locations Israeli forces require shelters, even basic ones such as dugouts, to provide some kind of cover, particularly when the troops are not in their armored vehicles. It could be added that the IDF needs to deceive the Hezbollah regarding the sites of the assembly areas, to divert Hezbollah fire to the wrong places.

Israeli airfields might be attacked by rockets. Preparing them to function under fire takes a substantial part of the time and training in those camps, according to Ron Ben-Yishai, national security correspondent and commentator on Ynet.[38] Maj. Gen. Amir Eshel, commander of the IAF, claimed in May 2014 that tests and checks conducted inside and outside the IDF proved that a barrage of rockets and missiles could not neutralize the IAF.[39] In April 2015 he said that he is "convinced that Israeli air bases will be the number one goal for Hezbollah as soon as such a conflict begins."[40]

The IAF has aircraft such as F-15, F-16, and AH-64 gunships. Each of those aircraft could reach nearby Lebanon to strike the Hezbollah, while only aircraft such as F-15I and F-16I could go all the way to Iran. Although the latter would prefer that the Hezbollah shoot its rockets at bases from where F-15Is and F-16Is would be scrambled to attack Iran, the Hezbollah might want to focus more on airfields that would serve as a springboard for air attacks against it.

Israel could remove many of its aircraft as far away as possible from Lebanon, i.e. from the Hezbollah's fire, by sending them to remote airfields in the south of Israel, such as Ovda, near the Egyptian border. From there aircraft could strike in Lebanon and then return to the relatively safe bases in the south of Israel. Helicopters could deploy elsewhere outside their bases, since they could land and take off from almost everywhere. Other Israeli corps could also relocate to temporary camps if the current ones became too exposed to fire from Lebanon. The gradual transfer of IDF bases, including airfields, from the center of Israel to its south would be a help in case of a war against the Hezbollah.

The Hezbollah is obviously quite familiar with the terrain of Lebanon. Some Israeli reserve troops would remember south Lebanon from their deployment there during their regular service in the 1990s. However, this being insufficient, the IDF has been training in similar topography to Lebanon, in areas such as the Galilee and the Golan Heights.

The IDF has also been training in urban areas, where Hezbollah's rockets are located. In IDF bases such as Elyaqim and Lachish, there are facilities that look like villages in Lebanon. Israeli troops have been learning how to avoid booby traps and use ropes and small robots.[41] The IDF also upgraded the cooperation between its corps. Israel's combat engineers would both clear routes from land mines and IEDs and pave new roads to bypass those that would be heavily mined, as was done in 2006.

Combat engineers would also prove helpful in underground warfare, in the bunkers and tunnels the Hezbollah dug in its strongholds. The fight there might turn out to be the peak of the campaign in Lebanon. In the Vietnam War, tear gas and special troops were part of the struggle in tunnels.[42] The IDF could implement those methods too. Hezbollah's men inside their bunkers might wear gas masks, but keeping them on for a long time under the ground would be a burden that would reduce their combat effectiveness. The IDF could also exploit its experience from handling tunnels in the Gaza Strip such as in the 2014 war.

Fire and maneuver

In the confrontation in November 2012 and particularly in the one in July-August 2014, the Iron Dome performed very well at intercepting rockets fired from the Gaza Strip. Israel claims that it requires between ten and 15 Iron Dome batteries "in operation at all times."[43] The lack of Iron Dome batteries during a war would result in less protection for the population, as mostly airfields and other key sites would require priority.

Furthermore, the IAF could not store enough Iron Dome missiles to shoot down all the rockets the Hezbollah can hurl at Israel. Iron Dome batteries might also be targeted by the Hezbollah. Some of Hezbollah's rockets might miss their objectives and land in open fields, but others might cause casualties and/or damage. Therefore, Israel's defensive approach, i.e. the Iron Dome, must be integrated with an offensive by land, air, and sea.

During its fight against the Hezbollah in the 1990s, the IDF initiated two major operations, one in July 1993 and one in April 1996, that brought limited results. As in those two operations, in the 2006 war the IDF sought to depend on firepower, not on maneuvers. The ability to produce lethal and accurate firepower from both ground and air pushed Israeli commanders to rely on what seemed a good measure to minimize their losses, but often it was not enough to accomplish the mission. In the 2006 war, Israel finally launched a large ground offensive, but it was executed too late and it exposed major defects in the IDF.

In recent years the IDF has been connecting its units in a secure C4I (Command, Control, Communications, Computers and Intelligence) network, which means the IDF could destroy many more targets per day compared with those in the 2006 war. The IDF has been investing a substantial effort to allow ground units to call in fire from various sources from the ground, air and sea.

In 2014 about 40 percent of artillery shells were "converted into precision shells that accurately strike targets as far as 40 kilometers away."[44] One Israeli F-16 could simultaneously hit more than ten targets in different objectives. In spite of this dramatic improvement, there is a debate among Israel's top brass about whether the IAF's devastating and precise firepower could replace maneuver in suppressing the firing of rockets.[45] According to Yaakov Lappin, the Jerusalem Post's military affairs correspondent, "it seems that military decision-makers have sided with those who believe that both elements are essential in a full-scale conflict, to ensure as speedy a victory as possible."[46] The 2014 war in the Gaza Strip showed that the IAF was not able to stop the firing of rockets at the Israeli rear or destroy all the tunnels the Hamas had.

The IDF could launch a "blitz invasion" into Lebanon although the fight there could require the IDF to depend on massive firepower and slow advance of the troops. In scenarios such as close combat in urban zones, firepower from the air and artillery could assist but not always, particularly under the ground. Bottom line: The IDF should be flexible enough to rely on firepower or maneuver or a combination of the two methods, according to the circumstances.

The Israeli ground units would have to cover other potential fronts like the Gaza Strip and the Golan Heights, yet many of them would probably be dispatched to Lebanon, including the IDF's elite armor and infantry units together with Special Forces. The IDF might be able to concentrate its forces against the Hezbollah. However, for Israel it would not make sense to send too many armored units into south Lebanon, with its narrow and often winding routes. The vehicles would be stuck in traffic and exposed to enemy fire, and only the force at the head of the columns could try to maneuver and fight back properly, as it was in the 1982 war. In the next war, the IDF should not overcrowd the roads in Lebanon while having sufficient numbers of units to carry out its assignments.

The firepower of the IDF's armored vehicles would help in close combat. Israeli tanks could launch their 120 mm APAM-MP-T cartridges and hit Hezbollah squads, such as those that possess antitank missiles . Actually, on the Lebanese front, most of the ammunition in Israeli tanks, APC (armored personnel carrier) and some of the artillery should be against infantry, not armored vehicles, let alone tanks, since the Hezbollah does not have them. Yet Israel's antitank projectiles such as the Spike missile could be exploited to crack fortified positions inside Lebanese villages and towns.

In the 2008–09 operation in the Gaza Strip, Israeli tanks had only half the ammunition they could carry. This improved their survival rates if they were hit by a powerful land mine. It also allowed them to carry infantry or wounded. Israel's best tank, the Merkava Mark 4, could hit a target 3.5 kilometers away from it on the first attempt 90 percent of the time. The probability grows to 98 percent in repeated fire.[47] This effectiveness might encourage the IDF to put less ammunition in the tank, which might improve their survival rates.

Israeli units such as the 401st Armor Brigade have the most protected tanks in the IDF, the Merkava Mark 4 with the new armored shield protective-active. This improves the tank's defense against antitank projectiles, as it was proved in battle in the Gaza Strip. The IDF should also rely on APCs with heavy armor: the Achzarit and the Namer since the old M-113 is too vulnerable to enemy fire. Forces such as Israel's first brigade, an elite infantry unit that has the Namer, could move at speeds of up to 40 kilometers per hour in order to reach their objectives fast. All those vehicles, including the most protected ones, would have to be careful of mines and IEDs.

In 2016 the Israeli navy has been preparing to assimilate the Barak 8 missile, aimed at intercepting Hezbollah's radar-guided missiles, which have a range of up to 300 kilometers. They put at risk Israel's gas drilling rigs, navy ships and the ports of Haifa and Ashdod.[48]

Israel's air offensive

The Hezbollah has several UAV but no fighters or bombers. Syria's air force, whatever is left of it following the civil war there, would probably not intervene in an Israeli campaign in Lebanon. The Syrian air force is no match for the IAF and Assad would not risk such a collision. Assad would not deploy antiaircraft batteries to face destruction in Lebanon either.

As a result of the war in Libya in 2011, "overestimating the impact of air power can mislead decision makers in future conflict."[49] Israel had already seen that in the 2006 war, yet in 2014 the IAF's ability to accurately attack targets was 15 times greater than in 2006.[50] The IDF, mostly from the air, could bomb Hezbollah's objectives in

Lebanon: its headquarters, ammunition dumps such as those that have rockets, Hezbollah's television station, etc. The IAF has bunker-buster bombs such as the GBU-28.[51] They could be dropped on Iran's nuclear sites and also on vital and well-protected targets in Lebanon such as the main headquarters and the bunkers where the Hezbollah keeps its most advanced long-range missiles.

Harsh weather might disrupt the IAF's operations such as collecting data with UAV while Hezbollah rockets might still be launched at Israel in such conditions. Israel's advance on the ground inside Lebanon might be delayed by weather too, but land units are less vulnerable than the air force in this sense.

In the 2006 war, the IAF cratered runways at Beirut's airport,[52] which was under the control of the Hezbollah. In the next war, if supplies could not be sent by land from Syria to the Hezbollah, then they could be delivered by air from Syria and/or Iran. In response the IAF might neutralize the Beirut airport and at least destroy the runways there.

Hezbollah's strongholds in Lebanon are in areas such as the Dahiyeh in the capital city, Beirut. The IAF would bomb that area, as in the 2006 war. The aim would be to put pressure on the Hezbollah to stop firing at Israel while punishing the group and trying to deter it in the future. The IDF could also strive to cut off Hezbollah's headquarters in Beirut from their units holding the rockets. Lack of communication might cripple the coordination inside the Hezbollah such as in receiving supplies or orders such as to focus on a certain target in Israel. Yet this disconnection could delay a ceasefire until every post the Hezbollah had would hear about it. Meanwhile its men there would continue to fight and fire at Israel.

The IAF is trained to bomb targets that are 250 meters away from an Israeli ground force while coordinating the strike directly with the commander of the land unit.[53] In the 2006 war, during a major battle in the Lebanese town of Bint Jbeil, the IAF got permission to drop a one-ton bomb about 100 meters from Israeli paratroopers, less than the minimal safety range.[54] In the next war, there might be circumstances in which the IAF would be permitted to once again ignore the rules in order to assist an Israeli ground force.

About 60 percent of the casualties of the Hamas during the 2008-09 confrontation in the Gaza Strip were from air attacks. It followed an Israeli ground offensive that forced Hamas's men to flee their shelters, thus exposing them. In Lebanon the IDF could use the same tactic.

The Hezbollah is believed to possess antiaircraft missiles such as the SA-8. Israeli aircraft, at low altitude, mostly helicopters and transport planes, could be jeopardized by antitank missiles due to their relative slowness.

The IAF has C-130 transport planes and CH-53 heavy helicopters. In mid-January 2012 and in late July 2013, the IDF's 35th Paratroopers Brigade parachuted in the course of a large exercise. In a war against the Hezbollah, such a vast vertical flanking could be used to reach several destinations deep inside Lebanon, including securing key points such as crossroads and bridges.

Should the IDF penetrate deep into Lebanon?

The IDF could reach all the way to Beirut, such as to the Dahiyeh, which is about 90 kilometers north of the Israeli border. Israel did that in the 1982 war, and it took about a week.[55] In 1982 the IDF faced the PLO, which was weaker than the Hezbollah is now. Furthermore, Israel's grim memory from the siege on Beirut in 1982 would probably nip in the bud an Israeli advance to Beirut or anywhere nearby.

The IDF might attack on a wide front for several reasons. One would be reaching as many rockets as possible quickly. Another would be succumbing to the demands of the rugged terrain in south Lebanon by exploiting any available road. A third reason would be the need to split the huge size of the Israeli force, which would probably amount to several divisions. A fourth reason would be Hezbollah's relative weakness as a military compared with the IDF and its lack of heavily fortified positions near the routes. Hezbollah's lines of defense would not require the IDF to gather a massive force at a certain point in a narrow front in order to gain a breakthrough. Also an Israeli advance inside Lebanon on a wide front would gradually push back the Hezbollah and its rockets, yet from sites deeper inside Lebanon the Hezbollah could continue to pound Israel.

An Israeli penetration deep into Lebanon might drastically reduce the launching of rockets into Israel. This maneuver would allow the IDF to develop momentum and to disrupt Hezbollah activities, such as delivering supply and reinforcements. Yet stopping Hezbollah troops from moving from one place to another could be difficult if they advanced in tiny groups at night, making use of the rough terrain they know well. The Hezbollah might also launch counterattacks but in a limited way due to Israel's overwhelming firepower and control of the air and sea. The Hezbollah could ambush small Israeli forces on a company level, particularly those from the logistic corps that were not armed, protected, and trained for combat, such as infantry or armor units.

UNIFIL (United Nations Interim Force in Lebanon), which was created in 1978, had about 15,000 troops in 2016. One of its missions has been to "assist the Government of Lebanon in securing its borders and other entry points to prevent the entry in Lebanon without its consent of arms or related materiel."[56] Yet for every UNIFIL soldier, there are about 10 Hezbollah rockets. UNIFIL was almost useless in this role, and its presence could also be a burden for Israel. In the next war, the IDF would have to avoid friction with UNIFIL and be cautious not to harm it as the battles raged between Israel and the Hezbollah. The IDF could outflank places in which the UNIFIL forces are based. If the Hezbollah fired from there at Israel or at Israeli ground units inside Lebanon, it would complicate the Israeli response. In a time of war, it seems it would be better for both Israel and the UN to evacuate all the UNIFIL troops as early as possible from Lebanon and at least from where the battlefield would take place.

In recent years the IDF conducted drills of crossing rivers and streams by using boats and bridges. This maneuver might be repeated in a war in Lebanon where the IDF would have to cross rivers. If the Hezbollah blows up the bridges before the IDF can prevent that, it would require building new bridges.

The IDF's 35th Paratroopers Brigade, together with other forces, including tanks, landed from the sea in Lebanon at the start of the 1982 war. The Israeli force created a bridgehead and later on advanced toward Beirut.[57] On other occasions the IDF landed across the Lebanese shoreline with much smaller forces for more limited purposes such as raids. Both methods would give the IDF an opportunity to surprise the Hezbollah in the next war. Yet the Israeli navy holds only a few landing crafts, so Israel's amphibious operations would be quite limited.

The Israeli navy, as a lesson from the 2006 war, will support ground units by firing at targets at the shore. The Hezbollah is expected to launch a barrage of missiles, rockets, boats full of explosives and suicide UAVs hoping to overwhelm the defense of Israeli vessels. In the 2006 war, a C-802 antiship missile hit and almost sank Israel's flagship, but on that occasion the crew was careless. In the next round, the Israeli navy would probably not underestimate Hezbollah capabilities.

The Hezbollah's strength

The Hezbollah maintains a vast network of tunnels to hide its forces and rocket launchers as well as secure communications, all in preparation for an Israeli strike. The Hezbollah has roughly 20,000 armed men, of whom 5,000 are elite fighters. The Hezbollah "can call on thousands more in a pinch; it has deliberately kept the size of its forces limited to ensure a high level of training and commitment."[58] It has between 20,000 and 50,000 "part time reserves."[59]

The Hezbollah would find it almost impossible to fight two fronts at the same time, one in Syria and another against Israel. The collision with Israel alone would put the Hezbollah in a hugely inferior position. The Hezbollah would need all its men in Lebanon. Iran, following an Israeli strike against it, would have to decide whether to allow Hezbollah units out of Syria to confront the IDF. If Iran insists that the Hezbollah fight on in Syria as well as against Israel in Lebanon, both Iran and Hezbollah might end up losing the war in Syria and in Lebanon too.

An Israeli major, the commander of an elite paratroopers unit, claimed in December 2012 that Hezbollah troops have basic infantry training and they are quite effective at firing mortars and antitank missiles.[60] They have been gaining combat experience in Syria in recent years while developing "command-and-control structure, including advanced telecommunications networks, the use of drones for reconnaissance, and the ability to maintain long supply lines—all tactics that its members think could play a central role in the next war with Israel."[61]

Nevertheless, clashing with Syrian rebels is not the same as confronting the IDF, which has immeasurably more capabilities. The Hezbollah might have learned the wrong lessons from Syria as far as its preparations to confront the IDF. In Syria the Hezbollah collaborated with Assad's forces, which have aircraft, heavy artillery and tanks. Their foe, the rebels, does not possess those weapon systems, especially not planes. If the Hezbollah clashes with the IDF, it would be the opposite situation. The Lebanese organization would not have tanks or aircraft while the IDF would have them. Furthermore, the Hezbollah got used to colliding with rebels who are far less trained and equipped, including in body armor, than Israeli troops.

The experience the Hezbollah acquired in Syria might drive its troops to initiate attacks. This would expose them to Israeli firepower, which is enormously more lethal than the light arms of Syrian rebels. This is why Hezbollah tactics such as in urban warfare that worked against Syrian rebels might not be that effective and even cost the Hezbollah dearly in a war against the IDF.

In a time of war, the Hezbollah might try to infiltrate into the north of Israel, aiming at killing Israelis and/or seizing some towns. Yet such an incursion would be a symbolic act for political purposes only, since any grip the Hezbollah got inside Israeli territory would not last long. Several dozen and even hundreds of Hezbollah troops who might manage to infiltrate into Israel, like via tunnels, could not push back a fierce Israeli counterattack that would be supported with massive firepower. The exception would be if the Hezbollah took hostages somewhere. This might delay the IDF from storming the building where they would be held.

The Hezbollah has between 30 and 200 fighters to protect the Lebanese villages and towns where the rockets are located. The IDF, striving for a short war,[62] could encircle and cut off Hezbollah objectives, avoiding a long siege, which might force the garrison to eventually surrender, but meanwhile they could fire rockets at Israel. The IDF would seek to break into the site as soon as possible and defeat the Hezbollah units deployed there.

However, Israel's top priority seems to be to destroy the rockets as fast as possible and at the lowest price to both the IDF and the noncombatants in those Lebanese villages and towns. The IDF might seek to achieve those goals by trying to convince Hezbollah troops to give up their rockets by simply withdrawing from their positions. It should be made clear to the Hezbollah troops that they need not become prisoners or even hand over their personal weapons but should just stay away from the rockets in their village or town and refrain from fighting the IDF when it seizes those rockets. After Israeli troops accomplished their mission, they would leave and not conquer the village or town. This would be another incentive for the Lebanese fighters to renounce the battle.

The IDF might also tell those Hezbollah men that its offensive in Lebanon was inflicting a substantial blow to the Hezbollah, i.e., the latter was losing and could not assist its troops. The IDF could further warn them that any resistance in their village or town would be crushed and the defenders would pay dearly unless they surrendered their rockets. Those messages should be delivered very distinctly. Hezbollah men might be aware of the danger in advance, but as the IDF approached, the threat would be concrete and imminent.

The combination of realizing the risks they faced, along with the way out that Israel might suggest—i.e., giving up the rockets in exchange for safety—might lead, in some places in Lebanon, to such a deal. In such cases Israel might not care too much if after the war Hezbollah men bragged that they managed to drive the IDF back from their town or village. If during the battles that site was not needed for other purposes, after destroying the rockets there, the IDF would retreat.

In the 2006 war, some Hezbollah troops wore IDF uniforms and held Israeli weapons. The Hezbollah might repeat this trick in order to confuse the IDF, particularly in close combat in villages and towns. The IDF should therefore consider giving its attacking units special uniforms to distinguish between them and their foe.

The human cost

In the 2006 war, Israel lost 119 troops and 43 civilians. In the next round, the Hezbollah would strike the Israeli rear, hoping to cause the maximum number of casualties. Israel has been aware, since it was established in 1948, that air bombardment, artillery, missiles, etc. could harm its civilian centers. However even now many existing shelters have been neglected, without sufficient protection or the basic conditions required for a long stay. Some Israelis don't have a shelter at all.

Besides that, some people would have to stay outside due to their jobs, for example, those providing emergency services. They might not reach a shelter every time there was an alarm of incoming rockets. Israel's military infrastructure, and even more its civilian infrastructure, that lacked protection would be exposed too. As the war went on, people would get used to procedures that would help secure them, but casualties could still happen. Those constraints would urge the IDF to seek a quick victory and at least to destroy the maximum number of rockets in the shortest possible time. On the other hand, rushing hastily might be costly if Israeli troops were not well organized or briefed before they attacked a certain objective in Lebanon.

On September 9, 2015, the state comptroller and ombudsman of Israel submitted a harsh report about the readiness of the Israeli rear. In case there is another war[63] such as with Hezbollah, lack of preparations and coordination between Israeli authorities might cost Israel dearly.

In the 2006 war, the Hezbollah lost about 500 men. In the next war—as far as the IDF perspective goes—Hezbollah fighters would be an obstacle on the way to the rockets' location. It could be argued that those Hezbollah men would have to be removed as early as possible by killing, capturing or driving them to retreat. The IDF would strive to inflict heavy casualties on the Hezbollah in order to retaliate, deter and delay the rehabilitation of this non-state organization after the war. Yet Israel's main goal might be to destroy the rockets, and harming Hezbollah fighters would be a secondary goal.

In the fight against the Hamas in the Gaza Strip in 2008–09, mistakes in directing Israeli fire caused both collateral damage and friendly fire. In 2013, the IDF military advocate general authorized targets in advance. He was led by the principle that according to the Geneva conventions, an objective is deemed a military one that could be attacked either because of its location or if it serves a military purpose, such as a civilian building that stores weapons. The IDF must warn the enemy population before a strike, limit collateral damage by choosing the proper weapons and ammunition and collect intelligence that would allow it to focus on the strike. The IDF would also try to encourage the Lebanese population to escape to the north of their country. This message would be delivered by taking over radio waves, dropping leaflets, etc. A senior Israeli officer said in March 2013 that Israel would try to give the Lebanese population sufficient time to leave their homes, "such that I hope non-combatants will be significantly fewer than 40 percent" of casualties.[64] In late January 2014, Maj. Gen. Amir Eshel warned that Israel would destroy thousands of Hezbollah's bases located in residential buildings in Lebanon, even if there were civilian casualties.[65] In early July 2015, a senior Israeli officer from the general staff said that the IDF might attack up to 10,000 targets inside urban areas in south Lebanon. This would require the evacuation of up to 1.5 million people, which he estimated could be done in only one day.[66] The IDF would therefore try to minimize collateral damage, but sometimes it would not be feasible. This would be the cost of turning large numbers of Lebanon's civilians into human shields of the Hezbollah and Iran because of their desire to harm and kill Israelis and cause severe destruction within Israel.

Notes

1 Arye Naor, *Cabinet at War*, (Israel: Lhb, 1986), 27–28.

2 On the emergences of the Hezbollah, see Joshua L. Gleis and Benedetta Berti, *Hezbollah and Hamas: A Comparative Study* (Johns Hopkins University Press, 2012), 38; Ahmad Nizar Hamzeh, *In the Path of Hezbollah* (Syracuse University Press, 2004), 15.

3 Carnegie Endowment for International Peace, April 2, 2014; http://carnegieendowment.org/2014/03/31/hezbollahs-last-ditch-battle/h6sa; Anthony Cordesman, *Peace and War: The Arab–Israeli Military Balance Enters the 21st Century* (London: Praeger, 2002), 403.

4 Hamzeh, *In the Path of Hezbollah*, 18.

5 Christopher O. Bowers, "Identifying Emerging Hybrid Adversaries," *Parameters*, Spring (2012): 43.

6 Amos Harel and Avi Isacharoff, *The Seventh War* (Tel Aviv: Miskal–Yedioth Ahronoth Books and Chemed Books, 2004), 156–158, 212.

7 Trita Parsi, *A Single Roll of the Dice* (Yale University Press, 2012), 1–4.

8 *The Washington Post*, July 23, 2016, https://www.washingtonpost.com/world/middle_east/ten-years-after-last-lebanon-war-israel-warns-next-one-will-be-far-worse/2016/07/23/58d7a6ca-4388-11e6-a76d-3550dba926ac_story.html.

9 *Maariv*, January 11, 2014, http://www.maariv.co.il/news/new.aspx-?pn6Vq=EE&0r9VQ=GHLHE.

10 Yoaz Hendel and Yaakov Katz, *Israel vs. Iran: The Shadow War* (Dulles: Virginia Potomac Books, 2012), 2–31.

11 On the Hezbollah ending its military resistance, see Hala Jaber, *Hezbollah—Born with a Vengeance* (Columbia University Press, 1997), 208.

12 Daniel Byman, A High Price—The Triumphs and Failures of Israeli Counterterrorism (Oxford University Press, 2011), 241.

13 *The Times of Israel*, January 18, 2016, www.timesofisrael.com/idf-chief-iran-deal-raises-specter-of-proxy-wars-with-israel/

14 *Haaretz*, June 15, 2016, http://www.haaretz.com/israel-news/1.725156.

15 Gordon Shmuel, *The Second Lebanon War—Strategic Decisions and Their Consequences* (Ben Shemen: Modan, 2012).

16 On the 1982 war, see Zeev Schiff and Ehud Ya'ari, *A War of Deception* (Tel Aviv: Schocken, 1984).

17 On the attack in 1992, see Moshe Arens, *Broken Covenant* (Israel: Yedioth Ahronoth, 1993), 292–93.

18 Benny Morris, *Righteous Victims—A History of the Zionist–Arab Conflict 1881–2001* (Tel Aviv: Am Oved, 2003), 594.

19 *Ynet*, August 10, 2003, http://www.ynet.co.il/articles/0,7340,L-272 2136,00.html.

20 Bruce Riedel, "Israel's Dilemma: If It Attacks Iran, Will It Also Have to Hit Hezbollah?" *Brookings*, February 9, 2012, http://www.brookings.edu/research/opinions/2012/02/09-iran-israel-riedel.

21 *Reuters*, November 20, 2013, http://www.reuters.com/article/2013/11/20/us-arms-israel-interceptor-idUSBRE9AJ0BC20131120.

22 About the 150,000 rockets, see the testimony submitted to House Foreign Affairs Committee hearing "Israel Imperiled: Threats to the Jewish State," a joint meeting held by the Subcommittee on Terrorism, Nonproliferation, and Trade and the Subcommittee on the Middle East and North Africa. David Makovsky, Ziegler Distinguished Fellow and Director, Project on the Middle East Peace Process, The Washington Institute for Near East Policy, April 19, 2016.

23 Jean-Loup Samaan, "From War to Deterrence? Israel-Hezbollah Conflict Since 2006" (working paper, the Strategic Studies Institute—SSI, May 2014), http://www.strategicstudiesinstitute.army.mil/pubs/display.cfm?pubID=1198.

24 *The Times of Israel*, June 14, 2016, http://www.timesofisrael.com/1200-rockets-a-day-in-next-lebanon-war-officer-warns/.

25 *Haaretz*, July 8, 2010, http://www.haaretz.co.il/misc/1.1210994.

26 *Reuters*, March 7, 2013, http://www.reuters.com/article/2013/03/07/us-israel-lebanon-hezbollah-idUSBRE92614520130307.

27 Riedel, "Israel's Dilemma."

28 *The Washington Post*, October 4, 2013.

29 *Haaretz*, July 8, 2010.

30 *Walla News*, June 1, 2012.

31 Avi Kober, *Israel's Wars of Attrition: Attrition Challenges to Democratic States* (New York: Routledge, 2009), 41.

32 Yaakov Lappin, "Only a Ground Offensive Will Defeat the Enemy, Says Senior IDF Source," *Jerusalem Post*, March 26, 2014.

33 BESA Center, February 1, 2015.

34 On IDF Strategy, see Michael Herzog, "New IDF Strategy Goes Public," (The Washington Institute for Near East Policy, August 28, 2015).

35 IDF Blog, May 6, 2014.

36 On the effect of budget cuts, see *Haaretz*, March 12, 2014. On this subject, see also IDF Blog, March 26, 2014.

37 *Ynet,* May 5, 2014, http://www.ynet.co.il/articles/0,7340,L-4516289,00.html.

38 *Ynet*, May 5, 2014, http://www.ynet.co.il/articles/0,7340,L-4515955,00.html.

39 *Walla News*, May 22, 2014, http://news.walla.co.il/?w=/2689/2748999.

40 *The Times of Israel*, April 2, 2015, http://www.timesofisrael.com/iaf-cheif-israel-still-mulling-preemptive-strikes-on-enemy-targets/.

41 *Haaretz*, March 6, 2012.*Ynet*, April 19, 2016, http://www.ynet.co.il/articles/0,7340,L-4793256,00.html.

42 On Vietnam, see Tom Mangold, *The Tunnels of Cu Chi: A Harrowing Account of America's Tunnel Rats in the Underground Battlefields of Vietnam* (Presidio Press, 2005). See also William C. Westmorland, *A Solider Reports* (Tel Aviv: The Ministry of Defense, 1979), 252, 275.

43 On the number of Iron Dome batteries, see The Congressional Research Service (CRS), June 10, 2015.

44 Lappin, "Only a Ground Offensive."

45 *Ynet*, May 5, 2014.

46 Besa Center, November 14, 2013, http://besacenter.org/perspectives-papers/israel-vs-iran-hizballah-axis/.

47 *Walla News*, May 29, 2014.

48 Yaakov Lappin, "Israel Navy Preparing for Hamas, Hezbollah Rocket and Missile Threats," *Jerusalem Post*, May 18, 2016.

49 SSI, June 28, 2013, http://www.strategicstudiesinstitute.army.mil/pubs/display.cfm?pubID=1161.

50 On the IAF's firepower in 2014, see Nrg, January 29, 2014, http://www.nrg.co.il/online/1/ART2/546/903.html?hp=1&cat=875.

51 On Israel's bombs, see Global Security, http://www.globalsecurity.org/military/systems/munitions/gbu-28.htm.

52 Andrew Chadwick, "The 2006 Lebanon War: A Short History Part II," *Small War Journal* (September 12, 2012), http://smallwarsjournal.com/jrnl/art/the-2006-lebanon-war-a-short-itstory-part-ii.

53 Ben Caspit, "Israel's Military Revolution," *Al Monitor*, April 17, 2014.

54 On 2006, see Amir Rapaport, *Friendly Fire* (Tel Aviv: Ma'ariv Books, 2007), 265.

55 On 1982, see Zeev Schiff and Ehud Ya'ari, *A War of Deception* (Tel Aviv: Schocken, 1984), 168.

56 UNIFIL (official site), http://www.un.org/en/peacekeeping/missions/unifil/mandate.shtml.

57 Mike Eldar, "Flanking from the Sea in the Operation 'Peace For Galilee'," *IDF Marachot* 299 (July–August, 1985): 26–35.

58 Atlantic Council November 17, 2014, http://www.atlanticcouncil.org/publications/hezbollah-in-a-time-of-transition.

59 The Washington Institute for Near East Policy, December 1, 2014, http://www.washingtoninstitute.org/policy-analysis/view/hezbollahs-syria-problem1.

60 *Ynet*, December 28, 2012.

61 *Foreign Policy* (March 3, 2016), http://foreignpolicy.com/2016/03/03/hezbollahs-death-valley/.

62 IDF Blog, IDF Archives, File Number 52/854/96, November 23, 2015, https://www.idfblog.com/blog/2015/11/23/idf-strategy/.

Ghani Abdel Mohamed El Gamasy, *The October War* (The American University in Cairo, 1993), 136.

63 The State Comptroller and Ombudsman of Israel (official site),

http://www.mevaker.gov.il/he/Reports/Report_347/75f5a4c9-3af4-48bc-87ca-332df7a53731/007-002-oref.pdf.

64 *Reuters*, March 7, 2013, http://www.reuters.com/article/2013/03/07/us-israel-lebanon-hezbollah-idUSBRE92614520130307.

65 *Reuters*, January 1, 2014, http://www.reuters.com/article/2014/01/29/us-israel-lebanon-hezbollah-idUSBREA0S1PS20140129.

66 On the Israeli senior officer, see *Walla News*, June 3, 2015, http://news.walla.co.il/item/2860317.

Chapter 3

Israel's Syrian Front

The cost of the Syrian civil war, by early 2016, might have been more than 470,000 dead while about half of the country's population was displaced. Israel might have to confront guerrilla and terror groups in the Golan Heights, a situation that might lead the country to consider collaborations with moderate Syrian rebels and minorities inside Syria such as the Druze.

The friction between Israel and Syria

Israel and Syria encountered each other in several wars up to 1982. Since then they have been continuously preparing for another war between them. Syria ran a proxy war against Israel in Lebanon in the 1990s and collaborated with Israel's sworn enemies, Iran, Hezbollah, and Hamas. In the 1990s and in 2008, there were peace talks between Israel and Syria that ended in failure.[1]

From the very beginning of the civil war in Syria in 2011, Israel has had an ambivalent approach toward Assad, not being quite sure whether his survival or demise would be preferable for Israel. In mid-May 2013, Amos Harel said, "Israel has no real interest in entering the whirlwind that is the bloody civil war in Syria or even taking sides."[2] Ironically both the Syrian rebels and Assad accused each other of collaborating with Israel.[3]

Charles Freilich said in late January 2014, "Both Israel and the international community face two terrible outcomes. One could lead to jihadists ultimately turning against Israel, and the other Syria becoming 'a virtual Iranian/Hezbollah client state.'" Eyal Zisser, an expert on Syria and Lebanon, added that "the West and Israel are not in a hurry to get rid of Assad."[4] Also "former US officials" made it clear "that Assad is no longer necessarily seen as the worst option for Syria's future."[5] Ehud Ya'ari, a Middle East commentator for Israeli television's Channel Two, said in early May 2014 that "there is a sharp debate within the Israeli defense establishment and the government over the extent of Israeli intervention in the Syrian fighting in order to prevent radical, Al Qaeda-affiliated militias from installing themselves adjacent to Israel's border on the Golan Heights."[6] Officially Israel declared that it does not support any of the sides. Meanwhile by fighting each other the different factions in Syria have been serving an Israeli interest. As long as the various rivals in Syria are busy with their Muslim foe, they would not turn against their Jewish enemy.

The United Nations Disengagement Observer Force (UNDOF) was established in 1974. Its mission is "to maintain the ceasefire between the Israeli and Syrian forces and to supervise the implementation of the disengagement agreement."[7] Following the fight inside Syria, at the border with Israel, near the UN troops, the latter almost completely stopped their patrols and they operated from within their posts. Syrian aircraft—involved in battles within Syria—sometimes ignored the rules of the armistice with Israel and bombed targets near the border, on the Syrian side. This caused the IAF to scramble its planes from Ramat David airbase to make sure there was no aerial penetration into Israel. On the ground, the IDF has made some changes in recent years. Its 36th division, which was in charge of the Golan Heights for decades, was replaced by the new 210th division, which focuses solely on day-to-day security. Regular infantry troops from the elite 1st and the 35th brigades were deployed in the Golan Heights instead of reserves. Israel also built a fence. The height of the fence is five and in some places seven meters, and it includes concertina wire. Those preparations will help protect the 20,000 Israelis who live in the Golan Heights, as well as the rest of the Israeli population, if terror or guerrilla detail penetrates from the Golan Heights deeper into the country.

On March 18 and 19, 2014, Israel bombed several targets inside Syria. The IAF has struck objectives in Syria since 2013, but the attack on March 18–19, 2014 was different in several aspects, starting with the reason for the Israeli attack, which was an assault against it. Israel is very sensitive to any kind of casualties. In recent years, there have been all kinds of minor incidents on the Golan Heights. Sometimes, they were the result of mistake, when mortar shells from the Syrian side, fired by struggling parties there, landed inside Israeli territory. On other occasions, Israel absorbed direct hits from explosive devices that were laid on the border. In those incidents, Israeli soldiers and civilians escaped without harm or only with minor injuries. On March 18, 2014, for the first time, four Israeli paratroopers were wounded, some of them seriously, by a roadside bomb.

Since 2011, when mortar shells fired from Syria, by either side there, hit Israeli territory in the Golan Heights, the IDF shot back at Syrian objectives. At the beginning, the Israeli fire was directed to the proximity of military camps in order to warn Assad and urge him to prevent any assaults against Israel. Assad could have restrained his military and maybe also his allies in Syria, such as the Hezbollah, but he obviously had more urgent issues on his plate. Stopping rebels from striking Israel, even if he wanted to, was no priority. Either way, from the Israeli perspective, Assad was responsible for any hostile action toward Israel that came from Syria, in spite of the civil war there.

Gradually, Israel increased the pressure on Assad when the IDF destroyed Syrian positions with artillery and spike anti-tank missiles. On March 18–19, 2014, the IAF attacked several Syrian targets. By doing that, the IDF threw into combat its strategic arm, the air force, and the Israeli response included more objectives than in other recent retributions near the border.

UN Resolution 2229 from June 29, 2015 concluded that the battles on the border in the Golan Heights "continue to have the potential to escalate tensions between Israel and the Syrian Arab Republic and to jeopardize the ceasefire between the two countries."[8] This reflected the situation there in recent years.

Over the years, Israel restrained itself when Assad sent thousands of rockets to the Hezbollah, which put the Israeli population at risk. This went on before the Syrian civil war, when the Syrian military was stronger and its troops could have focused on Israel. The latter dared to strike inside Syria in only a few cases before 2011. The most famous and important one was the destruction of the nuclear reactor in 2007, after Israel suspected that Assad was working to attain the bomb. In April 2003, Syria supported making the Middle East free of weapons of mass destruction.[9] By preventing Assad from producing a nuclear weapon, Israel helped to make progress on this crucial issue. The Israeli bombardment might have ignited a war, but it did not.

From 2013 to 2016, Israel launched air strikes inside Syria, aimed at stopping Assad from supplying advanced weapons such as anti-aircraft missiles to the Hezbollah. Israel attacked the deliveries, not the Assad regime itself, hoping to deter Assad from sending more weapons to Hezbollah without deteriorating the situation. Neither Israel nor Syria has any interest in escalating the tensions between them. Assad has been too busy with the rebels and has no need for another front. In spite of the ramifications of the Syrian civil war, such as the disruption of the quiet on the Golan Heights, Israel was prepared to tolerate this precarious situation as long as the different sides in Syria did not turn against it.

Hence, Israel did not admit to bombing deliveries of weapons from Syria to Lebanon. This approach made it easier for the Assad regime to avoid retribution against Israel. An Assad response could have increased the friction between Israel and Syria and led to war, which was against both of their interests. Israel was willing to risk a war, but only to destroy Iran's nuclear sites or maybe even Hezbollah rockets.

Each time Israel bombed inside Syria, the latter could have struck back hard, but in none of those assaults was the Israeli population put on high alert, and Israeli civilians were informed about the air attack inside Syria only when it happened. Israel did not warn its people, assuming correctly that Assad would not retaliate. It was a calculated risk. The Israeli government exposed its people to Syrian retribution in order to gain tactical surprise during the air strike and as part of denying Israel's bombardment of Syria. Israel wished to avoid a possible escalation and even a war. If it had called its people to go to shelters, not only Syria but Iran and the Hezbollah as well might have assumed that Israel was about to start a war against one of them and they might have opened fire at Israel.

On March 18, 2014, Israel took responsibility for the first time during the Syrian civil war for its air strike inside Syria. This time Israel probably assumed it could not deny its actions because of the scale and the location of its attack, near the border. In previous Israeli strikes inside Syria, there were fewer targets and/or they were far from the Golan Heights, some in the area of Damascus.

Israeli Prime Minister Benjamin Netanyahu, in his speech at the UN on October 1, 2015, warned, "Israel will continue to respond forcefully to any attacks against it from Syria ... Israel will continue to act to prevent the transfer of strategic weapons to Hezbollah from and through Syrian territory."[10] On April 11, 2016, he admitted that Israel had bombed deliveries of weapons from Syria to Lebanon.[11]

Assad's military options against Israel

Kenneth M. Pollack, senior fellow at the Saban Center for Middle East Policy, mentioned in August 2013 that the Syrian military "is a pale shadow of the prewar Syrian armed forces."[12] Major General Aviv Kokhavi, as the head of Israeli Military Intelligence, claimed in late January 2014 that the readiness of the Syrian military had never been lower.[13] In mid-2015, Assad had about 175,000 men, which included its military, militias, and foreign fighters like

Hezbollah.[14] In 2016, the Syrian military continued to struggle with many hardships. Syria's forces absorbed a lot more damage and casualties and lost much more land in the civil war than it had as a result of all its wars with Israel.

Martin Indyk, former Assistant Secretary of State for Near East Affairs, said in late September 2012 that the civil war destroyed Syria's "conventional capabilities and was steadily eliminating its ability to make war on Israel."[15] In July 2013, Amir Oren, a senior correspondent and columnist for Ha'aretz, argued that Syria's 1st Corps, which faces Israel in the Golan Heights, is not ready or trained for a full-scale war.[16] A collision with Israel could put Assad in grave danger due to Israel's military superiority. A series of devastating air bombardments would destroy Assad's air force, main ground units, etc. and by that allow rebels to close in for the kill. Assad, realizing his military weakness and fearing a massive Israeli retribution, might strive to limit the confrontation with Israel. However, such a war could get out of hand against the will of both sides.

In August 2013, Assad had less than a 100 aircraft in service, such as the rather old MiG-23.[17] In 2014, the Syrian air force was "not believed to pose a serious risk" to Israeli air operations .[18] Yet, in June 2015, Robert Ford, the U.S. ambassador to Syria from 2010 to 2014, claimed that Assad's air force "is still potent."[19] At the time Assad also had a "formidable air defense."[20] The IAF has more than 400 combat aircraft including advanced platforms such as F-16I. The IAF could shoot down any Syrian aircraft trying to infiltrate Israel. The interception should be done before Syrian planes manage to bomb any extremely vital areas in Israel, such as the city of Tel Aviv, which is about 200 kilometers from Syria, or the major city of Haifa, which is about 100 kilometers from Syria. A Syrian plane could cross those distances in a matter of minutes.

Theoretically, Syria could try to launch a massive air assault, which would increase the odds of some Syrian aircraft reaching their targets, but Assad would not risk his planes in such a mission. It is not worthwhile for him to pay a heavy price and risk a precious asset such as planes. Besides the symbolic meaning of the Syrian air force for Assad, his father having been the commander of that corps, aircraft are essential to fight against the rebels.

In May 2012, according to Brigadier General Itay Baron, Syria had about 3,000 missiles and rockets that have ranges from 70 to 700 kilometers.[21] They cover all of Israel. Major General Yair Golan claimed, in mid-September 2013, that the Syrian military had fired up to half of its long-range missiles.[22] Assad fired those missiles to achieve various goals, including demonstrating to his enemies that they were helpless against such an attack and striking facilities captured by the rebels so they could not use them.[23]

Some of Assad's arsenal is quite accurate, such as the SS-21, whereas other projectiles are less accurate, such as the FROG and the long-range Scuds. Assad gained combat experience in this field that might serve him against Israeli cities, including as part of Iranian retribution for an Israeli raid on its nuclear sites. The IDF, by monitoring the Syrian civil war, could learn about the performance of those missiles and rockets. Assad did disarm most of his chemical weapons (CW) but he could keep some missiles with unconventional warheads, albeit as the very last option.

If Syria pounded the Israeli rear with long-range missiles and rockets, some of them would probably miss their targets. Others might be intercepted by the Arrow and Iron Dome. The IAF would also bomb launchers of missiles and rockets, although hunting them inside Syria would not be easy. A similar case occurred in Western Iraq in 1991. During a future war that could last for weeks, the Israeli population would have to stay in shelters. Israel would absorb casualties and damage, particularly if it was not well prepared for such a challenge.

Major General Aviv Kokhavi mentioned in July 2012 that Assad had transferred a large part of his forces from the Golan Heights to Damascus since he was not concerned about a war with Israel.[24]

This meant that Assad had no intention of conducting a ground attack. Furthermore, Syria's military approach has changed since the late 1990s. It abandoned the option of unleashing a large-scale ground offensive in the Golan Heights and focused on striking the Israeli rear with indirect fire. In addition, the possibility of a massive Syrian ground attack has been significantly reduced due to an enormous upgrading of the IDF's ability to annihilate armored vehicles. Therefore, it seems very unlikely that Syrian forces would initiate any land offensive against Israel. The Syrian military is not up for this task, particularly as the civil war continues raging in the country and with it the destruction and wearing down of Syrian armored vehicles.

During the past decades, Syria could have initiated a very limited attack on the Golan Heights, aimed at seizing a military post, a settlement, or even just an empty space. It could have been a land assault or an airborne one. Preventing any penetration would have required the IDF to deploy many troops across the Golan Heights, not just near the border, since Syrian helicopters could reach sites all over the Golan Heights. Such an Israeli presence for an extended period of time would have been quite an economic burden, particularly if reserves had to be mobilized in mass. Instead, Israel has been relying on receiving early alerts from its intelligence community, enabling it to gather sufficient troops at the spot where the Syrian military would be expected to attack. In the worst-case scenario, the IDF would have conducted counterattacks to kick out any Syrian force that would have penetrated the Golan Heights. Assad could have also avoided any maneuver, firing just with artillery and rockets that cover all the Golan Heights.

In late September 2013, Syrian Foreign Minister Walid al-Moualem declared that his regime was determined to get back the Golan Heights.[25] The Arab peace initiative from 2002 called for negotiations and an Israeli withdrawal from several areas including the Golan Heights.[26] Lack of talks between Israel and the Arabs might have granted Assad legitimacy, at least among some

Arabs, to attack the Golan Heights if only in a symbolic way. Assad could have received support from Sunni Arabs. For Assad this goal might have been even more important than an actual strike against Israel. The Assad regime needed Arab endorsement following the blows to its image because of its brutality and mass killing of its Sunni population.

Syria has Yakhont anti-ship missiles[27] with sufficient range to hit vessels near the Israeli coast. Syria might use them to retaliate after an Israeli strike. Assad might also threaten to sink Israeli ships if the latter does not remove its maritime blockade on the Gaza Strip. Syria does not care about the Gaza Strip, especially after the rift between the Assad regime and the Hamas. Assad's goal would be to gather support among Arabs and to use it as leverage to pressure Arab states and Turkey not to help the rebels.

Israeli response to a Syrian assault

Overall, it seems that Israel hopes its deterrence and the tough situation Assad is in to would make Assad think twice before embarking upon a military adventure. In case Assad opens fire against Israel, the latter might avoid any retribution, particularly a major one, allowing Assad's enemies inside and outside Syria to do the work for Israel. Such a policy could undermine Israel's deterrence not only against Syria but against other foes such as the Hezbollah. Still, Israel might demonstrate restraint. The most decisive factor would be the number of casualties and the amount of damage Israel would absorb. This outcome would depend on the scale and accuracy of the Syrian fire and on the quality of Israel's anti-rocket and anti-missile systems, the performance of the Israeli Home Front Command, etc. The latter was examined in major exercises such as the ones that took place in early July 2015 and mid September 2016, simulating a missile attack on Israel. The 2014 confrontation in the Gaza Strip was also a certain test in this aspect.

If there are many civilian casualties in Israel, intentional on Assad's part or not, Israel might retaliate directly against the Assad regime and its inner circle. It would be similar to the assassination of leaders of terror and guerrilla organizations who were responsible for killing Israelis. This possible outcome might prevent Assad from attacking the Israeli rear and instead limit its assaults to the Golan Heights and/or solely to military targets. Such an approach might reduce the scope of the Israeli response against Assad. Both sides would probably strive not to be entangled in an unnecessary war.

The IDF conducted vast exercises on the Golan Heights in mid-September 2012, mid-March 2013, and mid-April 2014. Another drill there, on brigade level, was run in April 2015.[28] In April 2016, the IDF carried out a large-scale exercise on the Golan Heights that tested units like the 401st armored brigade.[29] Israel also built training facilities that looked like Syrian posts for its ground units.[30] In case of war, Israel would have probably tried to avoid a land offensive into Syria because of the possible cost of such a maneuver. Yet a ground attack would have been needed if Israeli air bombardments and artillery had not been able to suppress Syrian fire on Israeli objectives.

Assad's allies

Assad might try to compensate for his military inferiority by approaching Arab states for help. The Assad regime has had all kinds of alliances since 1970. Egypt and Iraq used to be its most powerful partners for war against Israel. Iraq, at least in the 1980s and up to 1991, and Egypt had the most powerful militaries among the Arabs. Syria made it easier for Egypt to attack Israel in 1973, and Iraq joined to help Syria in that war.[31] Although Syria felt betrayed in that war by Egypt, the latter remained a potential ally. The 1973 war also showed Syria the constraints of receiving assistance from Iraq, but it was still a vital component in any clash with Israel. Besides other disputes, Iraq and Egypt were also rivals of Syria in the struggle for hegemony in the Middle East. Yet, considering Israeli military might, Syria needed Egypt and Iraq.

Subsequent to the 1979 peace treaty between Israel and Egypt, the latter was no longer a part of a military coalition against Israel. Iraq became entangled in its own wars. First, it was the Iran–Iraq war from 1980 to 1988, when Iraq would not have been able to focus on Israel. Iraq built a huge military during that showdown, but instead of turning it against Israel, Iraqi troops attacked another small state in the Middle East, an Arab one, Kuwait. In the 1991 war, Iraq was defeated and lost much of its military capability, which was totally wiped out in the 2003 war. In addition, in 1991, the Soviet Union collapsed, which meant the dissipation of the military and political support Syria received from its Soviet patron for several decades. The Assad regime saw how Egypt's peace with Israel, Iraq's wars, and the Soviet meltdown deprived it of essential aid in a war with Israel.

Israel could have exploited Syria's low point and military inferiority, as it did in the past. In the 1967 war, Israel stormed the Golan Heights when Syria was left alone after losing its two allies, Jordan and Egypt.[32] In the 1973 war, Israel bombed Syria's rear, knowing the latter could not do the same on a similar scale. In 1981, Israel annexed the Golan Heights, but Syria did not go to war against the IDF. A year later, when Israel confronted Syria in Lebanon, Hafez al Assad received no help from Arab states. On other occasions, Israel avoided using its military edge against Syria, including when Syria supported guerrilla and terror assaults against Israel such as in Lebanon in the 1980s and 1990s.

Iran and Syria have been partners since 1979.[33] Since 2011, Israel has been finding the civil war in Syria as an opportunity to put pressure on Assad, unofficially, to make concessions such as to cut its ties to Iran and/or the Hezbollah. But Assad needed Iran to help him survive, relying also on Iran's proxy, the Hezbollah, to help him overcome the rebels in his country.

The involvement in the Syrian civil war of two of Israel's sworn enemies, Iran and the Hezbollah, helped Israel, for it diverted their attention from Israel . Instead of concentrating on Israel, they were forced to assist the Assad regime, a task that had become a burden for them. By 2016, it was estimated that Hezbollah had lost more than 800 fighters[34] whereas Iran lost almost 700 troops and militia men.[35] Iran also has a stake of billions of dollars invested in Syria and has absorbed criticism in the Arab world, a large part of which has been suspicions of its regional ambitions.

Iran might have hoped that even if Assad was toppled, Syria could continue to serve as both an Iranian base in the Levant and a frontline against Israel, besides the stronghold of the Hezbollah in Lebanon. Iran may also try to control a harbor on the Syrian shore of the Mediterranean Sea. Yet communicating with that port depends on the Suez Canal, i.e., on Egypt, unless the Iranian ships bypass all of Africa.

Although Syria did not intervene in the 2006 war and avoided opening a second front on the Golan Heights, the Hezbollah took a risk in 2012 and came to assist Assad. Syrian rebels, particularly Sunni radicals among them, might have turned against Hezbollah anyway after finishing with Assad. Yet, by attacking them on their land, the Hezbollah encouraged them to return the favor. Its strongholds in Lebanon came under several assaults, and the Hezbollah was accused of dragging Lebanon into the war in Syria. On the other hand, according to Middle East analyst Avi Issacharoff, the Hezbollah earned some advantages. Its men gained access to places around Syria, including the Golan Heights, and they received weapon systems from the Assad regime.[36]

In January 2013, following an Israeli strike in Syria, Iran's top nuclear negotiator, Saeed Jalili, claimed that Israel "will regret its aggression against Syria."[37] According to Bilal Saab, the executive director of the Institute for Near East and Gulf Military Analysis, "even a limited Israeli military intervention in Syria" could lead to a response from Iran and Hezbollah.[38] It would probably depend on the nature and scale of the Israeli operations. Iran might consider joining Syria in a war against Israel too much of a risk, particularly since Iran does not wish to provide Israel with an excuse to bomb its nuclear infrastructure. Furthermore, Iran might assume that Assad, even with substantial Iranian help, could not afford a war with Israel.

Iran sent Hezbollah to fight for Assad against the rebels, not Israel. Iran might assume that its Lebanese proxy should not jeopardize itself too much in a war against Israel, unless the latter attacks Iran's nuclear sites. Iran might agree to a limited contribution from the Hezbollah to a struggle against Israel from Syria, such as laying down IEDs at the border with the Golan Heights.

Iran might prefer an even more indirect way: striking a Jewish or an Israeli site somewhere around the world, as Iran and the Hezbollah have already done several times. Israel tries to foil such assaults. It could be argued that for Israel those kinds of assaults are less costly than the ramifications of war against Assad, even without the involvement of Iran and/or the Hezbollah.

Bernd Kaussler, an associate professor, and Keith A. Grant, an assistant professor, both from James Madison University, claimed that "Eastern Europe and Crimea are of vital strategic importance for Russia, whereas its distant besieged ally in Damascus offers diminishing returns in exchange for Putin's political and military support."[39] Yet, Russia assisted Assad by providing his regime with oil products and other merchandise along with weapons. Russia in return received access to the harbor in Tartus. Furthermore, since October 2015, Russian forces, mostly aircraft, have been officially fighting for Assad, so Israel has had to be careful not to collide with Russian planes.

Israel is a strong U.S. ally, yet it seems unlikely that Russia would seek a war between Israel and Syria as part of a Russian anti-American strategy. It would not be similar to the Cold War, when the Soviet Union sometimes had an interest in sparking a dispute between its Arab allies and Israel. Russia might assume that such a war would jeopardize the Assad regime. Nevertheless, if only for that factor alone, Russia might deliver weapons to Assad and give him diplomatic backup in case of a war between Assad and Israel.

Israel versus Syrian Islamic radicals

Israel's defense minister, Moshe Ya'alon, said in early July 2015 that the expansion of radical groups inside Syria might drag Israel into the fight there.[40] The various armed groups there might confront Israel whether Assad survives or not. Some of them have a presence near the border with Israel in the Golan Heights. They might attack Israel by relying on the low-intensity warfare they learned in the civil war. They might not only infiltrate into the Golan Heights but also develop hybrid capabilities by exploiting weapon systems captured from the Syrian military, such as artillery.

For Israel, this kind of confrontation is familiar from its clashes with the Hezbollah in Lebanon and the Hamas in the Gaza Strip. Yet the challenge would remain: finding and hitting guerrilla and terror groups, this time in Syria. This foe would generally be elusive since it would not rely on camps, facilities, or weapon systems such as planes that require airfields. Furthermore, Israel's hybrid enemy in Syria might be different from the Hezbollah and Hamas in its strategy, structure, and methods.

Israel would strive to avoid striking populated areas in Syria. Israel's hybrid enemies could exploit this by hiding among the Syrian people and firing their rockets from there. The Hezbollah and the Hamas, based on their philosophy that the end justifies the means, adopted this strategy, proving their willingness to let their population pay the cost of the war even if it was quite high. Since the Hamas and the Hezbollah were willing to absorb substantial casualties as their sacrifice for the cause, they expected their population to do the same and pay their share. Yet both the Hezbollah and the Hamas need the support of their people. In contrast, some radical Islamists in Syria, particularly those who came from outside Syria, might not have such ties and constraints. Many of those extremists might be indifferent to the suffering and the casualties among the local Syrian population. This would make it difficult to deter those groups. If Israel, as retribution for attacks on its civilians, bombs vital infrastructure in Syria, it could hurt Syria's civilians more than it harms Israel's foe there, driving part of the population to assist Israel's enemies.

If Assad survives, his anti-aircraft batteries could try to intercept Israeli planes attacking guerrilla and terror groups in Syria if Assad suspects the strike is against him. In former sorties against targets inside Syria, the IAF did not lose any planes, so in the future the IAF could rely on the same tactics that secured its aircraft in previous attacks. Since most of Syria is not under Assad's control anymore, his air defense could not cover those zones properly or even at all. Assad's aircraft could reach any spot in Syria, but they are no match for the IAF. Assad would rather keep his planes to bomb the rebels than jeopardize them in a clash with the IAF.

If Assad falls, the Hezbollah, which has been involved in the war in Syria, could be one of the main guerrilla and terror forces in Syria together with its allies there: the remains of the Syrian military, Alawite militias, Iraqi Shi'ites, Iranians, and local "volunteers." They would clash with Sunni groups. The Hezbollah and its allies would be under the influence of and even controlled directly by Iran, whereas their Syrian rivals might be supported by Saudi Arabia, Qatar, Turkey, and Jordan. Those four Muslim states and mostly Jordan could be a broker between the anti-Iranian forces in Syria and Western states—perhaps Israel too—in creating some kind of temporary, limited, and unofficial cooperation against their common enemy: the pro-Iranian camp in Syria.

CW and advanced weapon systems

Disarming Assad of most of his CW, an arsenal that was meant primarily to deter Israel, substantially improved Israel's security position. Assad continued to use CW by launching chlorine gas attacks inside Syria.

With Assad in power but especially if he is toppled, the different rivals in Syria would continue fighting to get hold of various assets. Syria does not have many natural resources such as oil, but apart from Assad's CW there are many weapons such as tanks and artillery, some of them quite advanced, such as anti-aircraft missiles. All of that could be grabbed, particularly if Assad is brought down. It could be worse than Libya after its 2011 upheaval, if there is no rule at all in Syria. Weapons that could deter internal foes would be essential for weak groups and those who might not trust their allies that much. For example, the Assad regime relies on the Alawites, who might fear retribution from all those who suffered under Assad.

In mid-2013, most of the Syrian CW were "transported to Alawite areas in Latakia and near the coast."[41] Some of it might be left in the hands of the Alawites. By holding CW, they could try to show their strength, so Iran and the Hezbollah would not abandon the Alawites if the latter loses controlling power in Syria.

The United States fears that advanced shoulder-fired anti-aircraft missiles delivered to rebels in Syria could end up in the hands of Islamic radicals, who would use them to shoot down civilian aircraft.[42] Many states, not only those around Syria, might be concerned about all kinds of weapons that are already in Syria. Containing the weapons sent from Syria would not be easy, considering its long and broken borders. This arsenal could spill out and jeopardize Western sites and interests in the Middle East and ignite civil wars both inside states that are Western allies such as Jordan and Saudi Arabia and within other states such as Lebanon.

If Syrian CW fall into the hands of radical Islamists, all of whom hate Israel, Israel should be ready to intervene in Syria. This might complicate and deteriorate even further the fragile and dangerous situation in Syria. It would be a challenge to locate and target the weapons there, including the CW, certainly if it is done from the air alone. Air strikes could destroy at least some of the weapons, mostly those that are exposed in bases or are more difficult to hide. Western planes might participate in this effort as well.

For Western states it could be kind of a test prior to a more important one. The situation in Pakistan is more precarious than in Syria due to its instability and possession of nuclear weapons. The United States and its allies would strive to prevent radical Islamists, whether groups or states such as Iran, from seizing any weapon arsenal, let alone a nuclear one, if Pakistan collapses into chaos.

Syrian armed groups would find it very difficult to maintain and operate weapon systems, mostly the more complex ones such as CW, anti-aircraft missiles, and aircraft. They would have to capture the manpower able to handle those weapon systems and convince or coerce them to serve a new boss. Even that might not be enough since there would be a need for spare parts, ammunition, and technical guidance for the weapon system, almost all of which came from Russia. Russia supports Assad and would probably not assist those who fought him, particularly not Islamic radicals who might have ties with their counterparts inside Russia.

Assad has managed to hold on, much longer than some in Israel and in Western states had predicted. Yet his tyranny might end anytime because of the assassination or the wearing down of his forces. If the Assad regime crumbles, its military might vanish completely, including its air defense. Its troops might assume that the threat on the ground would be much more serious than the danger from hostile aircraft. Those troops would probably stop fulfilling their professional role and prefer to return home immediately to protect their families from assaults by political and religious enemies and criminals, particularly since there would be no government to enforce any kind of law and order in the country. The air defense is a complex system that depends on radar, command and control centers, anti-aircraft batteries, etc., without one of which the system would be crippled and in Syria all the components would fall apart.

A total meltdown of the Syrian military would include not only the air defense but the air force as well. Syria's skies would be wide open. This change would pave the way for outside intervention by the international community, including Israel. These foreign powers would not have to worry that their aircraft would be shot down, except in cases of flying at low altitudes with aircraft such as helicopters, for they are at risk from even small arms. This concern would not prevent sending gunships and transport helicopters, either for raids or establishing a bridgehead useful for further operations. Seizing a Syrian airfield would be a jumping point for launching sorties around it, as part of the effort to destroy the Syrian arsenal.

As long as the Assad regime survives, Israel will continue avoiding massive strikes to destroy the arsenal there, but as soon as Assad loses control and Israel's foes such as the Hezbollah seize it, Israel might strike. In the meantime, in order to prevent a war with Assad, Israel would probably pursue its current approach of launching selective attacks when weapon systems are actually on their way to the Hezbollah in Lebanon.

Syria's open skies would be a convenient route for the IAF to fly to strike Iran. The same condition currently exists in Iraq, subject to change if and when the country rebuilds its air force and air defense. Meanwhile, the IAF would be able to fly from Israel through Syria and Iraq to Iran without running into many if any Arab anti-aircraft missile batteries or fighters. On such a mission, it would save Israel from the military and political hardships of dealing with other Arab states and their militaries like in Jordan. This would allow the IAF to focus on reaching Iran and fighting only with the Iranian air defense and air force.

Even if Iran produces a bomb, a post-Assad Syria could serve as a path for the IAF flying to Iran for the purpose of gathering intelligence and in a time of war for bombardments. In addition, in Syria, Israel might target Iranian supplies that would be sent by ground or air to Hezbollah in Lebanon or to Iranian supporters in Syria. The latter might be the spark for an Israeli–Iranian war.

Israel and Syrian Alawites, Druze, Christians, and Kurds

Syria has existed as a modern Arab state only since 1946. The dictatorial rule of the Assad family managed to hold the country together for more than 40 years, but Syria has always been an artificial state. A real chance for a stable government providing basic needs and securing the entire country without suppressing the population does not seem to be in the cards for this country. A solution might be to enable Syrian minorities to have some kind of autonomy, perhaps even a state of their own. Sunnis might control most of the country, whereas Alawites in the northwest, Druze in the southwest, and Kurds in the northeast form new entities.

Most Syrian Alawites live on the shores of the Mediterranean Sea, where they might create a fortified base if Assad is toppled. Access to the sea is vital for the Alawites but also for their rivals. The latter might wish to confiscate part of or even all of the shoreline from the Alawites in addition to trying to retaliate against them.

The Alawites would need help from Lebanon, which is south of their position and is populated by, among others, Alawites and the Hezbollah. The latter, together with its Iranian patron, might be interested in the harbors controlled by Alawites in Syria. For the same reason, Russia might assist the Alawites too. Russia and/or Iran could be the patron of the Alawites.

The Alawites might also try to approach nearby Turkey, which has more than 10 million Alawites, although most of them are not Arab such as those in Syria. The United States might not oppose such a step on the part of the Alawites, since Turkey is a member of NATO and is preferable by far to Russia, Hezbollah, and Iran having a foothold in Syria's shoreline. Israel would not carry much weight in this case, particularly if it seeks to reduce to a minimum its involvement in Syria. Being concentrated on Syria's shoreline, i.e., where there is no border with Israel, if the Alawites lose power, they will be less important to Israel and equal in this sense to the Iraqi Sunnis after the latter lost their rule in Baghdad.

Ygal Allon served as a major general in the IDF in the 1948–1949 war. Later on, he held several senior government positions, including minister for foreign affairs. He believed that Israel should strive to create a Druze state inside Syria that would be a buffer between Israel and Syria.[43] In the 1967 war, Israel conquered the Golan Heights. During the battles, the Israeli government rejected Alon's suggestion to conquer Jebel-al-Druze (the mountain of Druze), about 50 kilometers east of the Golan Heights, in order to create an independent Druze state. The Druze in the Golan Heights could have been part of a Druze state together with the Druze from Syria. The best chance for establishing such an entity was probably during the 1973 war when the IDF advanced inside Syria, yet north toward Damascus, not east in the direction of Jebel-al-Druze.

There are around 700,000 Druze in Syria, most in the south of the country. During the civil war, those Druze avoided joining the rebels for the most part. There was an idea that Israel would arm the Druze to fight for it.[44] There could be friendly ties between Israel and a Druze entity[45] in southwest Syria. There are about 130,000 Druze in Israel. They have been serving in the IDF, including in the top brass. A few reached the rank of major general. Some of them could be liaison officers between Israel and the Syrian Druze. In early July 2015, a senior Israeli officer from the general staff said that if Syrians, mostly Druze, were pushed by their foes to flee to the border, Israel would protect them.[46]

In 2014, Syrian Christians were "in most cases sympathetic" to Assad, but they did not want to be too associated with him in case the rebels eventually won.[47] The Syrian Christians, who were about 10% of the population in 2011, fear the day after Assad. By early 2015, Christians were less than 3% of the population there.[48] Their small number would prevent them from creating some kind of separate entity. Those Arab Christians would also have difficulty finding a patron in the Middle East, where Arab states are ruled by Muslims.

In Israel in recent years, there were a few hundred Arab Christians willing to volunteer to serve in the IDF or do national service. Although the idea of Arabs serving in the IDF, i.e., against other Arabs, is a sensitive issue, non-Israeli Arabs have been clashing with each other all over the region, and not only in recent years. Furthermore, Arab Christians in the IDF might not necessarily be required to fight but rather carry out missions such as coordination and communication aimed at helping Syrian Arabs.

Israel had collaborated with Arab Christians in Lebanon before and during the 1982 war against a nonstate organization there, the PLO Josef Olmert, an expert on Syria and Lebanon, claimed that "in many respects, the bitter Israeli experience in Lebanon ended its minority orientation. Here was a longstanding policy based on high expectations being put to the test, and the results were a far cry from those that had been anticipated."[49]

In addition, some claim that Syrian Druze and Syrian Christians hate Israel and do not want the state to exist.[50] Yet both Israel and those Syrian minorities might assume it would be worth their while to collaborate with each other. The Syrian Druze and Syrian Christians particularly should be aware that owing to their political and military vulnerabilities they must tolerate dealing with stronger forces they dislike.

There are hundreds of thousands of Sunnis near the border between Israel and Syria, some of whom—fearing anarchy and radical Islamists, including Sunni ones—may, for lack of a better option, collaborate with Israel. The latter has been concerned that ISIS or Syrian groups affiliated with Al Qaeda would strengthen their hold near Israel's border. Those radical Islamists are the common enemy of both Israel and many Syrians.

By 2016, more than 2,000 Syrians had been treated in Israeli hospitals, without being interrogated, so they could return to their country saying they had received quality care. Acts such as this might be a base for mutual understanding and cooperation between Israel and Syrians, mostly those close to the border.

In May 2014, Yoav Limor, a reporter of military affairs, claimed there were a lot of rebel organizations in Syria, which made it difficult for Israel to build a partnership with a group that would be both reliable and sufficiently stable. However, in the future it might happen.[51] In the same month, according to Ehud Ya'ari, rebels who attacked Assad's forces near the Golan Heights saw Israel as "having their back."[52] According to Jonathan Spyer in May 2014, "the evidence suggests that Israel has established contact with non-jihadi, Western supported rebel elements, with the intention of ensuring that the jihadists are prevented from establishing themselves along the ceasefire line on the Golan."[53] In February 2015, Jacky Hugi, the Arab affairs analyst of Israeli army radio, criticized the idea of such relations.[54] On June 29, 2015, Ya'alon claimed that Israel gives humanitarian assistance to Syrian rebels as long as "they don't get too close to the border, and that they don't touch the Druze."[55] Israel might collaborate with Syrian groups against their mutual enemy: Islamic extremists like ISIS and/or Assad and his allies, mostly the Hezbollah. Syrians would not fight for Israel, but they might fight for themselves and they might agree to receive economic and medical aid from Israel, along with weapons, ammunition, information, and maybe also training. Israel wishes to avoid deploying ground units in Syria, let alone on a large scale or for a long time. Israel would rather have its allies there do the fighting and at most be assisted by Israeli air bombardment. Western powers might adapt this concept too, by coordinating with Israel and their Syrian allies.

Anthony Cordesman, who holds the Arleigh A. Burke chair in strategy at CSIS, emphasized that Jordan "has become a key ally to the United States in dealing with Iraq and Syria."[56] Jordan denied "any involvement either in the supplying of armaments or the training" of Syrian rebels.[57] Nevertheless, Arab states such as Jordan might contribute to an unofficial and ad-hoc alliance between some Syrians, Western states, and Israel.

Jordan could train a local Syrian militia, as they did with Palestinian security forces. Jordan, similar to Syria, is also ruled by a minority that might be anxious about the disintegration of Syria, fearing its ramifications on the Hashemite kingdom. However, Jordan has vast experience in adjusting to complicated developments. A divided and therefore weaker Syria, having often been a rival and a threat to Jordan, serves Jordanian interests and facilitates gaining allies inside Syria with minimal effort.

The Kurds are the biggest minority in the Middle East without a recognized state of their own. It is estimated that there are more than 30 million Kurds, who are spread mostly in Syria, Iraq, Iran, and Turkey. In Iraq, they have already established a state within a state, including having a large militia. In Syria they are on their way to achieving that.

However, the Kurds, including those in Iraq, are still in a vulnerable position, since they do not have an actual state, access to the sea, or a solid alliance with powerful states. Militarily, they are inferior compared with some of their neighbors, like Turkey and Iran. In contrast, Israeli Jews, who are a much smaller minority in the Middle East, have had an official state since 1948, access to both the Red Sea and the Mediterranean Sea, close ties with great powers, mostly the United States, and one of the strongest militaries in the Middle East.[58]

Israel has maintained various ties with the Kurds since the 1950s. Ofra Bengio is a senior research fellow at the Moshe Dayan Center for Middle Eastern and African Studies. In mid-2014, she claimed that "it seems probable that the Syrian Kurds and the Israelis are sending feelers for possible cooperation. Some Kurdish groups in Syria evidently hope to gain Israeli support."[59] Israel might consider the Kurds as its local ally in east Syria, as part of an overall strategy toward Syria. It would give Israel a base to attack its rivals in that torn country, particularly if they confront Israel in southwest Syria, near the Golan Heights.

There has been an ongoing struggle between Turkey and the Kurds. Turkey seeks to help the Palestinians to fulfill their national aspirations but ignores the very same rights for the Kurds in Turkey and Arab states. The Turkish factor would be a major consideration in Israel's decision about how to handle support for the Kurds' cause.

Notes

1 Ma'oz Moshe, *Syria and Israel: From War to Peace-Making* (Tel Aviv: Ma'ariv Book, 1996). AvnerYaniv, Moshe Maoz, and AviKoberAvi, eds., *Syria and Israel's National Security* (Tel Aviv: Ministry of Defence, 1991). Anthony H. Cordesman with the assistance of Aram Nerguizian, and Lonut C. Popescu, *Israel and Syria: The Military Balance and Prospects of War* (Westport, Connecticut: Praeger Security International, 2008).

2 On Amos Harel see: Haaretz, May 16, 2013, http://www.haaretz.com/news/diplomacy-defense/israel-wants-no-part-in-syria-s-war-so-why-is-it-threatening-to-topple-assad.premium-1.524257.

3 *The New York Times*, February 25, 2014, http://www.nytimes.com/2014/02/25/world/middleeast/israeli-warplanes-strike-near-the-border-of-syria-and-lebanon.html?partner=rss&emc=rss&_r=0.

4 *Jerusalem Post*, January 27, 2014, http://www.jpost.com/Middle-East/Israeli-expert-on-Syria-The-West-and-Israel-are-not-in-hurry-to-get-rid-of-Assad-339456.

5 The Christian Science Monitor, January 5, 2014, http://www.csmonitor.com/World/Middle-East/2014/0105/Why-President-Bashar-al-Assad-s-rule-may-endure.

6 The Free Beacon, May 13, 2014, http://freebeacon.com/national-security/israel-treating-free-syrian-army-commander/.

7 UNDOF (official site) http://www.un.org/en/peacekeeping/missions/undof/.

8 United Nations Security Council (official site) http://www.un.org/en/ga/search/view_doc.asp?symbol=S/RES/2229(2015).

9 On that "the Syrian government is ready to sign a treaty under the

U.N.'s supervision to make the whole Middle East a zone free from all mass destruction weapons—nuclear, chemical and biological" see: CNN, April 17, 2003, http://www.cnn.com/2003/WORLD/meast/04/16/sprj.irq.un.syria/.

10 Algemeiner, October 1, 2015, http://www.algemeiner.com/2015/10/01/full-transcript-prime-minister-netanyahus-speech-at-the-united-nations-general-assembly-2015-video/.

11 Reuters, April 11, 2016, http://www.reuters.com/article/us-mideast-crisis-syria-israel-idUSKCN0X81TO.

12 Brookings, August 2013, http://www.brookings.edu/~/media/research/files/papers/2013/08/09%20military%20syria%20civil%20war%20us%20intervention%20pollack/08_pollack_syria.pdf.

13 Haaretz, February 1, 2014, http://www.haaretz.com/weekend/week-s-end/.premium-1.571578.

14 *The Times of Israel*, May 25, 2015, http://www.timesofisrael.com/syria-regime-preparing-for-partition-of-the-country/.

15 Brookings, September 20, 2012, http://www.brookings.edu/research/testimony/2012/09/20-israel-indyk.

16 Haaretz, July 7, 2013, http://www.haaretz.co.il/news/politics/.premium-1.2063847.

17 Brookings, August 2013, http://www.brookings.edu/~/media/research/files/papers/2013/08/09%20military%20syria%20civil%20war%20us%20intervention%20pollack/08_pollack_syria.pdf.

18 The Washington Institute for Near East Policy, May 23, 2014, http://www.washingtoninstitute.org/policy-analysis/view/syrian-air-defense-capabilities-and-the-threat-to-potential-u.s.-air-operat.

19 Middle East Institute, June 19, 2015, http://www.mei.edu/content/at/wringing-our-hands-and-endless-bombing-won%E2%80%99t-help-us-syria.

20 *Military Times*, August 3, 2015, http://www.militarytimes.com/story/military/pentagon/2015/08/03/us-air-strikes--syria/31069911/.

21 Haaretz, May 23, 2012, http://www.haaretz.com/news/diplomacy-defense/idf-israel-in-range-of-nearly-65-000-hezbollah-iran-syria-rockets.premium-1.432012.

22 Reuters, September 18, 2013, http://www.reuters.com/article/2013/09/18/us-syria-crisis-israel-idUSBRE98H09H20130918. The Israeli Defence Minister Moshe Yaalon said the same. See: Reuters, November 20, 2013, http://www.reuters.com/article/2013/11/20/us-arms-israel-interceptor-idUSBRE9AJ0BC20131120.

23 The Washington Institute for Near East Policy, April 26, 2013, http://www.washingtoninstitute.org/policy-analysis/view/the-syrian-regimes-use-of-surface-to-surface-missiles.

24 Haaretz, July 17, 2012, http://www.haaretz.co.il/news/world/1.1778430.

25 Jerusalem Post, September 30, 2013, http://www.jpost.com/Middle-East/Syrian-FM-Syria-formally-confirms-mission-to-restore-Israeli-occupied-Golan-Heights-327477.

26 EliePodeh, "Israel and the Arab Peace Initiative, 2002–2014: A Plausible Missed Opportunity," *Middle East Journal* 68(4)(Fall 2014):584–603.

27 *The New York Times*, May 17, 2013, http://www.nytimes.com/2013/05/17/world/middleeast/russia-provides-syria-with-advanced-missiles.html?pagewanted=all&_r=0.

28 On the drill see: INN, April 2, 2015, http://www.inn.co.il/News/News.aspx/296083.

29 Ynet, April 20, 2016, http://www.ynet.co.il/articles/0,7340,L-4794185,00.html.

30 Ynet, April 20, 2014, http://www.ynet.co.il/articles/0,7340,L-4510980,00.html.

31 On the 1973 war see: AviKober, and ZviOfer, eds., *The Iraqi Army in the Yom Kippur War* (Tel Aviv: Ministry of Defense, 1986).

32 On the Israeli attack in 1967 see: Matitiahu Mayzel, *The Golan Heights Campaign June 1967* (Tel Aviv: Ministry of Defense, 2001).

33 Jubin M. Goodarzi, "Syria and Iran: Alliance Cooperation in a

Changing Regional Environment", *Middle East Studies* 4 (2) (January 2013): 31–59.

34 On the number of casualties see the Washington Institute for Near East Policy, February 22, 2016, http://www.washingtoninstitute.org/policy-analysis/view/hezbollah-fatalities-in-the-syrian-war.

35 *The Telegraph*, May 10, 2016, http://www.telegraph.co.uk/news/2016/05/10/almost-700-iranian-troops-killed-in-syria-to-preserve-bashar-al/.

36 Walla News, March 20, 2014, http://news.walla.co.il/?w=/13/2731029.

37 *Huffington Post*, January 31, 2013, http://www.huffingtonpost.com/2013/01/31/syria-and-iran-threaten-r_0_n_2589528.html.

38 *Foreign Affairs*, October 28, 2013, http://www.foreignaffairs.com/articles/140225/bilal-y-saab/the-incredible-shrinking-buffer.

39 *The National Interest*, May 26, 2014, http://nationalinterest.org/feature/could-the-arab-spring-create-new-balance-power-the-middle-10529?page=4.

40 *The Times of Israel*, June 9, 2015, http://www.timesofisrael.com/dempsey-says-israel-will-not-lose-regional-military-edge/.

41 On the CW in the hands of Alawites see Reuters, August 28, 2013, http://www.reuters.com/article/2013/08/28/us-syria-crisis-chemical-idUSBRE97R0GJ20130828.

42 On the fear about shoulder fired anti-aircraft missiles see The Wall Street Journal, February 14, 2014, http://online.wsj.com/news/articles/SB10001424052702304703804579382974196840680.

43 Avi Shlaim, *The Iron Wall* (Tel Aviv: YdiotAhronot, 2005), 332-333.

44 On Israel arming Druze see: The New York Times, April 16, 2013, http://www.nytimes.com/2013/04/16/opinion/syrias-forgotten-front.html.

45 FPRI, October 2013, http://www.fpri.org/articles/2013/10/partitioning-syria.

46 On the Israeli senior officer see: Walla News, June 3, 2015, http://news.walla.co.il/item/2860317.

47 The Strategic Studies Institute (SSI), May 5, 2014, http://www.strategicstudiesinstitute.army.mil/index.cfm/articles/What-Will-Happen-to-Syrias-Christians/2014/05/05.

48 Foreign Policy May 1, 2015, http://foreignpolicy.com/2015/05/01/is-bashar-al-assad-finished-for-real-this-time-again-syria.

49 On Olmert see: Joseph Olmert, "*Israel and Alawite Syria: The Odd Couple of the Middle East?*," *Israel Journal of Foreign Affairs* 7(1) (January 2013):18, http://israelcfr.com/documents/7-1/7-1-3-JosefOlmert.pdf.

50 Syria Comment, November 13, 2013, http://www.joshualandis.com/blog/druze-militias-southern-syria/.

51 On Yoav Limor see: Israel hayom, May 2, 2014, http://www.israelhayom.co.il/article/178691.

52 The Washington Institute for Near East Policy, May 14, 2014, http://www.washingtoninstitute.org/policy-analysis/view/the-heating-battle-for-southern-syria.

53 Gloria Center, May 30, 2014, http://www.gloria-center.org/2014/05/a-most-discreet-intervention/.

54 Al Monitor, February 26, 2015, http://www.al-monitor.com/pulse/originals/2015/02/israel-syria-rebels-jihad-sunni-shiite-golan-heights.html#.

55 *The Times of Israel*, June 29, 2015, http://www.timesofisrael.com/yaalon-syrian-rebels-keeping-druze-safe-in-exchange-for-israeli-aid/.

56 Center for Strategic International Studies (CSIS), March 17, 2013, http://csis.org/publication/need-new-realism-us-saudi-alliance.

57 The Congressional Research Service (CRS), August 27, 2016, http://www.fas.org/sgp/crs/mideast/RL33546.pdf.

58 *The National Interest,* October 2, 2013., http://nationalinterest.org/commentary/no-friends-the-kurds-9161.

59 Ofra Bengio, "Surprising Ties Between Israel and the Kurds," *Middle East Quarterly*(Summer 2014), http://www.meforum.org/3838/israel-kurds.see also: ShlomoNakdimon, *Broken Hope* (Tel Aviv: Yediot Aharonot, 1996). Eliezer Tzafrir, *Ana Kurdi* (Tel Aviv: Ma'ariv Book Guild, 1998).

Chapter 4
Israel versus the Palestinians

Israel has been dealing with the Hamas and the Palestinian Authority (PA) on various levels, including the military one. The Hamas has been Israel's most vicious foe among the Palestinians.

Israel and the Hamas in the Gaza Strip

Israel conquered the Gaza Strip in the 1956 war, left it after a few months, and then seized it again in the 1967 war. In the early 1970s while occupying Gaza, Israel had to deal with a rebellion there and with an uprising from 1987 to 1993. Following the Oslo accords, Israel retreated from most of the Gaza Strip in 1994 and ran a low-intensity war there from 2000 to 2005. In 2005, Israel withdrew completely from the Gaza Strip and the PA took over.

In 2007, using brutal force, the Hamas grabbed the Gaza Strip from the PA, i.e., Fatah, the movement that controls the authority and is the main rival of the Hamas within the Palestinian camp. Since 2007 the Hamas has been initiating numerous assaults against Israel, mostly by firing rockets and mortar shells on Israeli towns and villages. Israel retaliated on several levels. In November 2012, there were somewhat restrained military clashes. In December 2008, confrontations reached their peak, as well as in July and August 2014.

The Hamas does not recognize Israel's right to exist, whereas Israel does not consider the legitimacy of Hamas as a representative of the Palestinian people. Nevertheless, since 2007, due to their constraints both sides have reached unofficial understandings and have accepted the current reality. The Hamas wants to take over all of Israel but cannot seize even a tiny part of it owing to the military superiority of the IDF. Israel could conquer the Gaza Strip in a matter of days but prefers to refrain from doing so, considering the negative military, political, and economic ramifications of such an act.

The Palestinian public has been seeking unity, following the cold war between the PA and the Hamas. Considering the tension between the factions, the odds of such unity surviving very long and/or having a significant impact are not very great to begin with. The deep hatred and difference of interests between Hamas and the Fatah undermine it. It is probable that the PA will continue to represent the Fatah, whereas the Hamas will keep running the Gaza Strip.

Seizing the Gaza Strip?

The Hamas "is likely to help any peace treaty fail,"[1] i.e., to foil talks between Israel and the PA. The Hamas has also been trying to increase its influence in the West Bank by using its supporters there. Yet, Israel and the PA have been pretty successful in blocking the Hamas from gaining too much strength there. The Hamas has kept the PA out of the Gaza Strip, although the PA still retains some of its men there. The PA officially tolerates the presence of Israel while rejecting the Hamas as a legitimate ruler of the Gaza Strip. For the PA, Hamas has always been a sworn enemy if not the most dangerous one.

The IDF could exploit its overwhelming military superiority to seize the Gaza Strip. Gazans who have been loyal to the PA could contribute by collecting intelligence for the IDF and even participating in the battles, fighting in separate sectors, not side by side with the IDF. In spite of the well-known collaboration between the PA and the IDF in the West Bank, the PA might fear that a joint operation in the Gaza Strip might be regarded as a betrayal in the eyes of many Arabs, including Palestinians. The PA's re-entry into the Gaza Strip might be seen as a reward for the PA at the expense of its own people, those whom their leadership is supposed to protect. The PA might be viewed politically as depending on the IDF.

As a result of all these complications, any official military collaboration between Israel and the PA in recapturing the Gaza Strip would be unlikely. Another option would be Israel assisting covertly by arming and training a Palestinian force to recapture the Gaza Strip, by landing from the sea, for instance. Such a plan, however, might end as the fiasco of the Bay of Pigs in 1961.

The IDF, with or without the PA, could conquer the Gaza Strip, but in the confrontations between the IDF and the Hamas, in 2008–2009 and 2014, Israeli forces, having seized areas inside the Gaza Strip, did not linger there. The IDF renounced conquering the entire Gaza Strip and bringing down the Hamas, wishing to avoid heavy casualties among its troops and collateral damage due to fighting in one of the most crowded areas in the world.

Furthermore, it might be easier to seize the Gaza Strip than to hold it, although the PA leaders might accept Israel handing it over to them, in spite of their political concerns about such a move. The biggest problem of the PA might actually be a military one. The PA might face tough opposition from the remains of the Hamas and other guerrilla and terror groups like the Islamic Jihad and the Popular Resistance Committees. The PA would need the IDF in the Gaza Strip even more than in the West Bank. A failure of the PA, even with Israeli aid, or lack of any attempt to restore the rule of the PA to begin with, would leave Israel with the need to handle the Gaza Strip alone, once again.

In September 2015, a report on United Nations Conference on Trade and Development (UNCTAD) assistance to the Palestinian people showed the huge economic problems of the Gaza Strip such as in regard to lack of water, electricity, and jobs.[2] Israel allowed humanitarian aid to be sent to the Gaza Strip, including during the confrontations of 2008–2009 and in 2014 as well. If Israel conquered parts of that area, it would be responsible for the provisions of necessities (water, food, medical, and other basic services) to hundreds of thousands of people while it was in charge of them. As stated, the Gaza Strip is already in a bad shape, and if during the battles infrastructure was damaged, let alone destroyed, the situation there would deteriorate. Israel does not need that enormous burden. Israel's troubles would worsen if it conquered all the Gaza Strip and took responsibility for about 1.8 million Palestinians. Israel would also face incursions not only from the Hamas but from other organizations seeking to drive it out. Israel would probably have to deal with both international criticism and growing tension with Arab states, including those that have peace with Israel, Egypt, and Jordan. If Israel did invade Gaza, it would strive to escape all those hardships by leaving the Gaza Strip as soon as possible.

In a future confrontation, after Israel withdraws from the Gaza Strip, Hamas might come back with a vengeance. However, if Israel, albeit unintentionally, struck the Hamas too hard and then retreated, the Gaza Strip would be left in total anarchy. Egypt, which has plenty on its plate, might refuse to take charge, and the PA could be too weak to rule over Gaza. Lack of infrastructure and government facilities—obliterated during the war—would make it difficult for anyone to maintain some form of authority there.

Under those circumstances, different Palestinian factions, including those that are associated with Al Qaeda and ISIS, would clash with each other and with Israel at the same time. An Israeli retribution would be more complicated to carry out this time, since there would be no one officially in charge after the Gaza Strip was split between the various factions. The IDF would need to be careful and to strike back only against the exact group that attacked Israelis. Sometimes the boundaries between the different zones in the Gaza Strip would be vague. Furthermore, civilians would be at risk. A major Israeli penetration deep into the Gaza Strip might cause most and even all the factions there to turn against the IDF.

The battle on, under, and above the fence

There is a fence around the Gaza Strip, which serves as both a border and a defense line for Israel. The alert systems and the readiness of Israeli troops stationed there have prevented infiltrations deep into Israel, including suicide bombers, who struck Israel mostly in the 2000–2005 confrontation. Over the years, there have been many Palestinian attempts to harm Israeli troops near the fence, by laying down an IED, ambushes, etc.

On some occasions the Hamas managed to dig tunnels under the fence and surprise Israeli troops. A case in point occurred on June 25, 2006, when an Israeli tank crew was attacked, two of its members were killed and one was captured. In the confrontation of 2014, the IDF discovered dozens of tunnels inside the Gaza Strip. Some of them stretched for a few kilometers and ended inside Israel. The Hamas launched many assaults from the tunnels, mostly from those inside the Gaza Strip, and in some cases managed to surprise Israeli troops and inflict upon them serious damage.

Another way to bypass the fence was to shoot over it. Around 6,000 rockets and mortar shells were launched from the Gaza Strip into the south of Israel in 2005–2008,[3] which led to the 2008–2009 confrontation. That major clash ended with a shaky ceasefire, which was broken many times. For a year leading from the clash in November 2012 until November 2013, about 50 rockets and mortar rounds were launched at Israel from the Gaza Strip, mostly not by Hamas but by other guerrilla and terror groups.[4] In mid-March 2014, following the continuous fire from the Gaza Strip, Israeli Strategic Affairs Minister Yuval Steinitz and Foreign Minister Avigdor Lieberman called to retake the Gaza Strip. Steinitz aimed at a temporary seizing of that area in order to wipe out the terror groups and retreat, as it was done according to him during the confrontation in the West Bank in 2000–2005.[5]

The Hamas often attempted to restrain not only its men but other radical Islamic organizations in the Gaza Strip such as the Islamic

Jihad and the Popular Resistance Committees. These groups frequently disobeyed the Hamas by firing at the south of Israel. It was not always clear if and when the Hamas stopped, ignored, or even permitted those assaults on Israel. This uncertainty imposed upon Israel the need to estimate against whom to retaliate: the ruler of the Gaza Strip or renegades inside it. Nonetheless, Israel has held Hamas responsible for every assault that comes out of the Gaza Strip. This went on until the next confrontation in the war of July–August 2014, when more than 2,000 rockets were fired at Israel. The Hamas jeopardized its people by provoking Israel and deploying its rockets near civilian sites, which made it difficult for the IDF to avoid collateral damage.[7]

Since the war of 2014, there has not been much fire at Israel because Hamas has not only avoided that but even tried to stop other groups from launching rockets. Hamas must also provide its people with their basic needs if it wishes to survive as a ruling entity. Blaming Israel for Gaza's dire straits would not cut it for long. There have been signs of unrest there in recent years. Tough and sometimes deadly suppression might not be enough to keep the Hamas in power, as other Arab rulers have learned firsthand since 2011.

For Israel, the Hamas is the lesser evil considering alternatives like the Islamic Jihad. Similarly, the PA is considered by Israel to be less problematic than the Hamas. Generally, the Hamas is viewed as a more hostile version of the PA. Israel is aware that both the PA and the Hamas dream of seizing all of Israel's lands; accordingly anti-Israel incitement is rampant and ubiquitous in their media and educational systems. However, it seems that Israel wants those two Palestinian entities to be powerful enough to prevent guerrilla and terror assaults against Israel from their soil while not presenting a significant threat to Israel. The latter strives to achieve this goal by using economic pressure and direct negotiations with the PA while participating in indirect talks with the Hamas, applying economic pressure, and engaging in military operations.

In fact, Israel has a bigger fish to fry: dealing with the Iranian nuclear project. Getting ready to confront the Hezbollah has been another priority. The Golan Heights area has known some unrest, and Israel has also been making an effort to block the smuggling of advanced weapons from Syria to the Hezbollah in Lebanon. For Israel, handling the Hamas in recent years was perceived as a relatively minor issue. However, the 2014 confrontation demonstrated the danger the Hamas posed to Israel mostly due to its rockets and tunnels. Another confrontation, maybe even more severe than the last one, might occur there again, against the will of one or both sides, owing to a random escalation of some incident, miscalculations, etc.

Egypt and the Hamas

Although the current regime in Egypt opposes the Hamas, there could be public pressure in Egypt calling to support the Palestinians in the Gaza Strip if during a future confrontation between Israel and the Hamas many of them would be hurt. In past wars, Arabs assisted other Arabs who had been rivals, including by dispatching troops. A good example was when Jordan came to help Syria in the 1973 war, three years after Syria had invaded Jordan. Egypt might also choose such a move for reasons irrelevant to the Palestinians, for instance, diverting public opinion in Egypt from troubles at home.

Egypt also wishes to get rid of the demilitarization in Sinai. Egypt might exploit a war between Israel and the Hamas to deploy hundreds of tanks all over the peninsula including near the Gaza Strip, claiming that the purpose of this entire move is to protect the Palestinians. In response, Israel would probably warn Egypt to pull back its forces. In the worst case, it might lead to a confrontation between Israel and Egypt.

In April–May 2014, Egypt benefited from the agreement between the PA and the Hamas, which was supposed to unite the Palestinians. Egypt was seen as protecting the interests of the Palestinians, although Egypt continued to show its hostility toward

Hamas. This policy was demonstrated again in the confrontation between Israel and the Hamas in 2014.

Egypt, due to its enormous internal problems, might be destabilized and even end up as a failed state, leading to a free flow of weapons, such as rockets, from Sinai to the Gaza Strip. This might also happen if the Egyptian policy toward the Gaza Strip changes. In response, Israel could conquer the part of the border between the Gaza Strip and the Sinai, on the Palestinian side, known as the Philadelphi Route/corridor, about 14 kilometers long. In the 2000–2005 confrontation, holding that area was a tough mission for the IDF due in part to the friction with Egypt. Sometimes incidents erupted between the two states. If they occur there again in the future, they might cause an escalation that could bring on a serious crisis between Israel and Egypt.

Instead of redeploying near the border with Egypt, Israel might pick a place along the Gaza Strip to build a barrier blocking smuggling to most of the Gaza Strip, while avoiding direct and dangerous friction with Egypt. Such a location would also be sparsely populated with noncombatants as compared to the areas near the border with Egypt, to reduce the probability of collateral damage. The barrier should be positioned in the narrowest point in the Gaza Strip, making it much difficult to breach. The depth of this barrier must be such to frustrate Palestinian attempts to bypass it from below through tunnels. Israeli air bombardments, artillery, and tanks could fire, including from outside the Gaza Strip, hitting those trying to infiltrate through the barrier. Those measures might reduce the need to deploy Israeli troops inside the Gaza Strip, which would put them in harm's way even if they were in well-protected strongholds. Mines and other obstacles could also help strengthen the barrier. Noncombatants, trade, etc. could carry on between the two separate parts of the Gaza Strip through gates in the barrier, supervised by Israel, replacing the border with Sinai, over which Israel has no control.

In such a case, the Hamas could launch its rockets from the

southern side of the Gaza Strip, obtaining rockets from Sinai, but then Israel would gain more time to alert its people and send them to shelters. Rockets launched from the north of the Gaza Strip, closer to Israeli objectives, would not allow that. Shooting from the South, the Hamas would also have less ground to fire from, which would increase the odds of finding and destroying rockets before they were launched at Israel.

The approach of Arab states and organizations toward the Hamas

In the 2014 confrontation in the Gaza Strip, Saudi Arabia, the UAE, and Jordan saw the Muslim Brotherhood (MB) as "the Islamist group from which Hamas sprang, just as threatening as Iran."[8] This accounts for their refraining from intervening in the clash, as they might do in a future confrontation. They might tacitly encourage the Israeli military to do to the Hamas what the Egyptian military did to the MB in Egypt in July 2013, i.e., topple its rule. Other states in the region, mostly Iran, Turkey, and Qatar, might express their support of the Hamas and condemn Israel for its actions against the Hamas, as they did in the confrontation of 2014.

The Hamas helped train Syrian rebels,[9] who might assist the Hamas in a future confrontation against Israel. Syria is hundreds of kilometers northeast of the Gaza Strip, and its rebels would not send men or weapons, but they might open a second front against Israel. Some rebel outfits are deployed near the Israeli border in the Golan Heights. Those armed groups are not very strong and even if Assad fell, they could not transform into a modern military, in spite of the weapons they would seize in Syria. It takes more than that to build an advanced military machine. With the arsenal and skills those groups possess, they could try to help the Hamas mostly by infiltrating into the Golan Heights and shooting there, but they would not strike the Israeli rear. For the Hamas, it would not replace the support of states like Syria and Iran, although when the Hamas struggled to hold its own against the IDF, as in 2008–2009, its Iranian and Syrian patrons did not open another front against Israel.

Hamas, Iran, and Syria

Daniel Byman, the research director of the Saban Center for Middle East Policy, mentioned that "with ties to groups like Hamas, Iran was also able to establish itself as an important actor against Israel—always a popular cause in the Middle East."[10] Iran has been striving to turn the Gaza Strip into a fire base against Israel as it did with the Hezbollah in Lebanon, as part of deterring Israel from attacking Iran's nuclear sites.

Notwithstanding an Israeli raid, Iran might seek a confrontation between its proxies in the Gaza Strip and Israel. The Iranian aim would be to divert the international attention from Iran's nuclear project, particularly if Iran runs into a crisis with western powers. A showdown in the Gaza Strip might also ignite a war between Israel and Egypt, two of the most powerful states in the Middle East, which stand in the way of Iran's regional ambitions.

The Gaza Strip as a fire base against Israel would be essential for Iran, since a war with Israel would be conducted mostly in the air, considering the distance between the two countries. Iran would wish to cripple the IAF. Rockets that would be fired from the Gaza Strip at Israeli airfields could obstruct sorties coming out of those bases and perhaps even reduce their number. The second type of targets would be Israeli cities, as part of an Iranian retribution for Israeli raids in Iran, even if the IAF restricts its attacks to military sites only. Rockets and missiles with a range of several dozen kilometers that would be launched from the Gaza Strip would put at risk at least a million civilians in the south of Israel such as in Be'er-Sheva, a city that has about 200,000 people.

The Red Sea has been a part of a logistic pipe that stretches from Iran to the Gaza Strip. The IDF has been disrupting this Iranian effort by bombing stockpiles in Sudan as in the strike that took place in late October 2012. In early March 2014, in the Red Sea, Israel captured the Klos-C, a ship that carried weapons from Iran.

This kind of struggle between Israel and Iran goes back at least 14 years as in January 2002, when the IDF captured the ship Karine A in the Red Sea. The vessel was supposed to deliver to the PA about 50 tons of arms including rockets with a range of 20 kilometers.[11] The identity of the Palestinian organization to which Iran has been delivering weapons has changed over the years. What seems to stay the same has been Iran's desire to harm Israelis and to undermine the chances for a peaceful solution.

The Hamas, even if it rebuilds its ties with Iran, might avoid any collaboration with Iran against Israel due to the ramifications. The Hamas might remember the vast destruction Israel inflicted on the Gaza Strip in 2008–2009 and in 2014. Furthermore, Hamas's leaders might fear for their rule and for their lives. The Hamas believes in sacrifice, but as a tactical approach, not as a strategic goal, certainly not one the Hamas is willing to commit for other groups or states. There is a limit to what the Hamas would absorb for any ally or patron, important as they might be.

Hamas has had an alliance with a major Iranian partner, the Assad regime. However, the latter could not have used the struggle between Israel and the Hamas as leverage to regain the Golan Heights during the talks with Israel. In the 1990s in Lebanon, Syria could have exploited its influence over the Hezbollah as an advantage in the negotiations for a peace treaty between Israel and Syria to return the Golan Heights to Hafez al Assad. If Bashar al Assad, his son, had had in the Gaza Strip the same effect his father had in Lebanon, he might have been able to coerce the Hamas to stop confronting Israel as a part, official or not, of an agreement between Israel and Syria.

Syria did not help the Hamas during the confrontation of 2008–2009, when the Hamas was in a tough spot. The Hamas returned the favor in 2011 during the uprising inside Syria. Hamas might have also calculated that even if the Assad regime survived, it would be weak and too busy with internal affairs to assist the Hamas; therefore, helping Assad would not really benefit the Hamas. The latter acted very aggressively against its own opposition in the Gaza Strip, sometimes by implementing lethal measures, as Assad did in Syria. In reality, the suppression in the Gaza Strip has been on a much more limited scale compared with that in Syria, but that is due solely to the fact that the Hamas has not faced a similar uprising.

In April 2002, during a major Israeli operation in the West Bank, the Hezbollah launched almost 1,000 rockets and mortar shells and some antitank missiles at Israeli strongholds near the border with Lebanon.[12] In 2002, the Hezbollah expressed solidarity with Palestinian fighters, but in the confrontation of 2008–2009, the Lebanese organization avoided helping the Hamas. Matthew Levitt, the director of the Stein Program on Counterterrorism and Intelligence at the Washington Institute, claimed that the massive Israeli offensive against the Hezbollah in the 2006 war deterred it from assisting the Hamas in the Gaza Strip during the 2008–2009 confrontation.[13] The Hamas and the Hezbollah then shared the same patrons: Iran and Syria. Those two states probably wished to avoid any entanglement of the Hezbollah in that clash, since a front in Lebanon between the Hezbollah and Israel could have dragged Syria and/or Iran into the fight. Syria and Iran wanted to save the Hezbollah for another fight, in case Israel attacks Syria and/or Iran. In this sense, the Hamas was kind of expendable, and it might have understood that point.

After the Hamas refused to assist Assad in 2011, Iran cut almost all its aid to the group.[14] Iran kept its ties with another nonstate organization in the Gaza Strip, the Islamic Jihad, which might try to start a fight with Israel, hoping to drag the Hamas into it. Iran might even consider using Israel to punish the Hamas. Iran might seek the downfall of the Hamas, in order to pave the way for a group more loyal to Iran, i.e., the Islamic Jihad. Either way the Islamic Jihad seeks a clash with Israel due to its extreme ideology. This radical Palestinian group does not care much about ramifications such as hurting the population in the Gaza Strip, since Islamic Jihad leaders have never experienced ruling over a populated area and do not bear the responsibility for the people.

Military aspects of a confrontation in the Gaza Strip

The main military advantage of the Gaza Strip is its location, a kind of deep wedge, 40 kilometers long, inside the south of Israel, which makes it a springboard for attacks such as firing rockets. Until mid-2014, the Hamas produced hundreds of rockets with a range of 80 kilometers, enough to reach the Tel Aviv area, together with thousands of rockets with a range of 20–40 kilometers. Many of them were fired in the confrontation of July–August 2014. The blows in the Tel Aviv area, even without causing casualties or much damage, were a propaganda victory for the Hamas, considering the strategic and symbolic value of the Tel Aviv area. Hamas, which continues to produce rockets, would try to hit Tel Aviv again in the next round.

Israel has an active defense against rockets, the Iron Dome, which proved itself in the war of 2014.[15] In February 2016, the Israeli navy successfully tested the C-Dome system, a sea-based version of the Iron Dome, aimed at defending Israel's offshore gas drilling rigs from rockets launched by the Hamas.[16] Israel's passive defense relies on building fortifications for the troops and shelters for the population. However, providing such cover for all the soldiers and citizens would take time and would be very expensive. A vast land offensive into the Gaza Strip might be unavoidable. In the 2014 confrontation, the occupation of a tiny part of the Gaza Strip by Israel reduced but did not stop the shooting on targets inside Israel. In the future, the IDF might seize all the Gaza Strip or a major part of it in order to minimize this threat to Israel.

In mid-2015, the IDF's exercises were "conducted to prepare for a full conquest of the Gaza Strip."[17] In keeping with its doctrine and based on the lessons learned from the 2014 war, the IDF would aim for a quick victory, particularly since the Israeli population would be exposed to fire from the Gaza Strip. Achieving victory would require close co-operation between the Israeli corps, a balance between firepower and maneuver, comprehensive training in advance and high morale. The IDF has also invested heavily in upgrading the gathering and delivery of information to its combat units. The aim is to allow the officers to know in advance and during the battle itself where the enemy is located.

At the beginning of the 2008–2009 confrontation, Israel managed to surprise the Hamas and might do it again. The latter could not afford to be on full alert all year long against a major and sudden attack of the IDF from the air, land, and sea. The IDF might also try to shock its foe with a massive first strike, as in the confrontation in November 2012. Again, the main aims would be disrupting the command and control of the Hamas by killing top commanders and destroying its strategic arsenal, the rockets.

There is a dispute regarding the number of Palestinians killed in the confrontation of 2008–2009 and how many of them were fighters or civilians.[18] The IDF then, and again in confrontations in 2012 and 2014, made a major effort to reduce unnecessary casualties among Palestinian civilians, relying on precision-guided munitions. Yet, in 2014, the substantially increased use of artillery by the IDF, which was not as accurate as aircraft, brought collateral damage. In the next round, the IDF should reconsider firing unguided artillery shells inside urban areas. Either way avoiding harming the Palestinian population would be a challenge for the IDF if the Hamas once again coerced its people to serve as human shields, in order to provoke world public opinion to pressure Israel to halt the offensive.

In June 2014, the Hamas had about 45,000 police officers, and fighters.[19] The IDF has about 170,000 regular troops. Against a relatively small organization like the Hamas, deploying mostly regular troops, without mobilizing many reserve units, could be sufficient. That would make it easier for the IDF to train for the fight. Reserves are called for exercises for only a few weeks each year, at best, whereas the regulars are available throughout the year. It is easier to plan a surprise attack with regulars, since reports about reserves getting mobilized en masse might reach the media, including the social networks, which would put the Hamas on alert.

The Hamas has some military problems similar to the ones plaguing Israel particularly from 1949 to 1967. Israel and the Gaza Strip are relatively long and narrow. From 1949 to 1967, Israel's major cities and infrastructure were only several kilometers from the border with Jordan. In the Gaza Strip, all the main cities including Gaza City are a few kilometers from the border with Israel. A swift IDF penetration into the Gaza Strip, like the one the Arab forces might have done into Israel before 1967, could have ended the war quite quickly. Any retreat would have immediately put Israel's vital areas in 1949–1967 at high risk. The same goes for the Hamas. The latter also could not deploy its forces around the clock near the border because of operational, logistical, economic, and political constraints. That too resembles Israel's situation during 1949–1967.

Even if the Hamas gets enough time to gather its men, not all of them are well trained and armed. This force would not be sufficient to block the IDF from reaching every spot in the Gaza Strip. The border there is an open area, without any natural obstacles, and the Hamas lacks resources to create artificial barriers strong enough to stop a large-scale Israeli offensive. Tunnels and underground bunkers could help the Hamas, as in 2014, but they would not be sufficient to hold back the IDF. At most, the Hamas could seek to inflict as many casualties as possible on the IDF while trying to delay the Israeli attack.

The Hamas might hope that international pressure would eventually halt the IDF before it managed to conquer all of the Gaza Strip and topple the Hamas. If those are the Israeli goals, the IDF should strive for a massive and sudden offensive from land, air, and sea at the beginning of a war with the Hamas.

Another option, which has never been implemented by the IDF in the Gaza Strip, is an amphibious operation somewhere along the 40-kilometer coastline of the Gaza Strip. A landing, particularly on the shores of Gaza City, might surprise the Hamas from its rear since the latter would probably focus on the other direction, on the land borders with Israel. That is where the IDF attacked in all previous wars. Until now Israel's navy has been used mostly to shoot at targets in the Gaza Strip and to cast a blockade on its shore, but not to send troops to storm the beaches. The IDF has a few landing crafts but together with other boats, smaller ones, it might be sufficient to launch an attack. Considering the moderate strength of the Hamas and the lack of defenses on the shores of the Gaza Strip, even a relatively limited Israeli force could create a bridgehead.

The IDF might land units from the air, particularly during a surprise attack when the Hamas is unprepared. Israel's helicopters could approach every spot in the Gaza Strip, but they would be exposed to fire from the ground. The IDF wishes to avoid a "Blackhawk down," i.e., helicopters shot down, crashing into a hostile and crowded city. This would complicate the rescue of the Israeli crews and the troops within. Yet, if this happens as part of a massive Israeli invasion into the Gaza Strip, the troops in those helicopters might be saved in time.

Since the confrontation of 2008–2009, the Hamas has developed military capability by investing in training and acquiring antitank missiles.[20] This activity proved useful in some cases in the 2014 confrontation, and the experience the Hamas gained would help it in the next round. Its men might also repeat shooting shoulder-fired anti-aircraft missiles, which would put at risk Israeli aircraft at low altitudes.

The top priority of IDF's Gaza Division in 2016 is to prepare counter-tunnel measures, i.e., to detect and destroy tunnels, which could be used by the Hamas to infiltrate into Israel.[21] The Hamas could do that as a response to an Israeli offensive or as part of launching a first strike against Israel.

A UN commission that studied the 2014 war published a report on June 22, 2015. It criticized both sides for putting civilians at risk. The report called "upon all parties to fully respect international humanitarian law and international human rights law, including the main principles of distinction, proportionality, and precaution."[22] This part of the report made it seem as if the commission assumed the next clash in the Gaza Strip would be just a matter of time.

A confrontation in the West Bank

In January 2013, Amos Harel estimated that a Palestinian uprising, a third Intifada, is unlikely.[23] Shimon Shamir, the first Israeli ambassador to Jordan, said in mid-February 2013 that "the situation in the West Bank is explosive. A third Intifada might well erupt there sooner or later."[24] In early July 2013, John Kerry, U.S. Secretary of State, warned that if the talks between the PA and Israel failed, a third Intifada might occur.[25] A report by one of the Palestinian security forces assumed in 2013 that there was a high probability of a third Intifada if the negotiations with Israel collapsed.[26] Eventually, the talks led to a dead end but there was no outburst.

Ben Caspit emphasized in January 2014 that a few radicals, including Jewish ones, creating a provocation could ignite a confrontation.[27] Shlomi Eldar is a columnist for Al-Monitor's Israel Pulse. According to him, senior figures in the Israeli security and military establishment assumed in May 2014 that the PA had no interest in another Intifada. According to that evaluation, most of the Palestinian public does not want to be entangled in another violent struggle, because of the bitter memory from the 2000–2005 confrontation. Yet, Eldar claimed "it seems that fuel vapor encompasses once again the West Bank skies. One little spark can set it on fire."[28] Khaled Elgindy, a fellow at the Saban Center for Middle East Policy, added in June 2014 that "like their counterparts in neighboring Arab states, young Palestinians have grown increasingly disaffected with their leaders, whether secular or Islamist, and are increasingly drawn to 'revolutionary' solutions."[29] In July 2014, the unrest in the West Bank might have ignited a third Intifada.[30] Yet, at that time Ehud Yaari assumed that the Palestinians did not want it, since they remembered the ramifications of the last collision with Israel.[31]

Following the unrest in Jerusalem in October–November 2014, there was concern about the third Intifada.[32] In January 2015, Itamar Rabinovich claimed that the chances of an uprising loom "larger as the political and diplomatic stalemate continues and popular pressure accumulates."[33] In April 2015, according to Efraim Inbar, "a Palestinian strategic miscalculation, leading to the eruption of another round of violence, is a possibility that Israel cannot ignore."[34] In the same month, Shadi Hamid and Daniel Byman assumed that "a third Intifada remains unlikely."[35]

In July 2015, Steven Simon claimed that "there is growing risk of a violent uprising in the West Bank."[36] In early September that year, Moshe Maoz assumed that Israel might be at the start of an Intifada.[37] The unrest in early October in Jerusalem was called a "personal Intifada,", since most of the Palestinians did not want a conflict.[38]

Anthony Cordesman claimed in November 2015 that both sides "seem willing to let the situation move towards another—and possibly far more violent—Intifada."[39] Former Chief of Staff and Defense Minister Shaul Mofaz warned in early January 2016 that a collapse of the PA would force Israel to take over all of the West Bank. "An additional Intifada under such circumstances will not be long in coming, and this is therefore a starkly negative event—if it happens. Israel and the Palestinians have no interest in the manifestation of such a scenario."[40] In early February 2016, the Awrad Research Institute did a survey of 1200 Palestinians, which showed that 42% were in favor of another uprising. [41] Some called the wave of Palestinian assaults that started in October 2015 an Intifada.[42] Overall, there is prolonged tension between the Palestinians in the West Bank and Israel due to political, security, and economic issues, which might lead to a major confrontation.

The first big uprising in the West Bank and the Gaza Strip after 1967 was in 1987–1993. The IDF used nonlethal measures such as rubber bullets and sometimes also live fire to disperse violent protesters. Its troops also conducted chases after those who threw stones and fire bombs, and they put suspects in detention, ran patrols, etc. This kind of police activity was a Sisyphus cycle.[43] The next major confrontation between the two sides, in 2000–2005, was from the start a low-intensity war. The Palestinians had light arms and rockets. The IDF confronted them mostly with infantry, tanks, and aircraft. A third large-scale collision might be like that of 1987–1993 or 2000–2005 or a combination of the two, such as mass demonstrations heading toward Israeli settlements in the West Bank, together with ambushes of Israeli vehicles on the roads with fire bombs, guns, or IEDs.

The IDF plans to rely on intelligence and forward command, allowing freedom of action to its units, cooperating with Palestinian security forces, containing terror activity, and keeping the day-to-day routine of the population. The IDF has measures to suppress demonstrations, by using gas grenades, stun grenades, and "Skunk," which throws a mist that sticks to clothes. If the confrontation was an actual low-intensity war, the IDF would shoot back with its arsenal, mostly infantry and tank fire.

Bruce Riedel is a senior fellow and the director of the Brookings Intelligence Project. He mentioned that "Israel has a long history of fighting terrorism and has exceptional capabilities to counter terror threats ... The Israeli intelligence and security services like the Shin Bet are among the best in the world."[44] Those services proved their worth during the conflict with the Palestinians, particularly in foiling assaults or discovering who planned and carried them out if they were executed. Those skills would be necessary again if there was another confrontation in the West Bank. The PA might oppose such a face-off and try to stop clashes between Palestinians and the IDF. In the West Bank, unlike in the Gaza Strip, Israel's units could reach every area without an invasion, simply by approaching the Palestinian security forces, following the usually effective cooperation with them. PA security forces can prevent too much friction between Palestinian demonstrators and Israeli troops. But this could change. The PA might stand aside and even join and initiate skirmishes.

On May 15, 2014, there were fierce demonstrations in the West Bank. The insufficient number of PA security forces in those events led to an escalation that cost the lives of two Palestinians among the demonstrators. PA security forces' concern has increased, since their people blamed them for collaborating with Israel. This happened as the talks about an agreement between Israel and the PA reached a dead end.[45] In early June 2014, Ron Ben Yishai emphasized that since the Palestinian security forces are less active, their Israeli counterparts have to do more by themselves. This raised the odds in favor of an outburst, following a demonstration or a detention of Palestinians that could go wrong.[46] If there is a series of wild demonstrations against Israelis in the West Bank, and the PA security units do not fulfill their duty, the crisis might deteriorate and become more violent. The IDF might be forced to adopt a tougher approach, which could trigger further escalation, making a struggle that might have started as an uprising look more and more like a low-intensity war. Under such circumstances as in 2000–2005, PA security forces might not only avoid assisting the IDF but even fight against Israel. The PA's security forces have 30,000 men.[47] Some of them gained a lot of experience in the West Bank. They might exploit their knowledge and weapons to conduct deadly assaults.

At the beginning of the 2000–2005 confrontation, Israel had a dilemma: Was the PA, particularly its leader, Yasser Arafat, involved in guerrilla and terror attacks against Israelis? And if so, to what extent? If in the future, areas under PA control serve again as a jumping board to assault Israelis, the Israeli government might not hesitate too much. Israel might re-occupy large parts and even all of the West Bank. It could be the end of the PA, which is probably well aware of the danger to its very existence as rulers of the West Bank if the outburst gets out of control and/or Israel retaliates too strongly against the PA.

If there is another confrontation between the Hamas and Israel, the PA might stay out of it as it did in 2008–2009, 2012, and 2014. On the other hand, the Hamas might show solidarity with the PA if the latter confronted Israel. The Hamas calculation would probably be to use Israel as a scapegoat, blaming it for all the misfortunes and internal hardships in the Gaza Strip to divert frustration from inside the Gaza Strip toward Israel.

Hamas and the PA as well hope that Israel would strike its foe in the Palestinian camp. Yet, both the PA and the Hamas would probably assume that even if their internal opponent was crushed, they could not take over its territory. The PA is too weak to run the Gaza Strip and Israel would not allow Hamas to seize the West Bank.

Notes

1 The Council on Foreign Relations (CFR(, March 21, 2014, http://www.cfr.org/peace-conflict-and-human-rights/critical-hamas-success-israeli-palestinian-peace-treaty/p32628.

2 United Nations Conference on Trade and Development, September 14–25, 2015, http://unctad.org/en/PublicationsLibrary/tdb62d3_en.pdf.

3 Israeli Security Agency (official site) http://www.shabak.gov.il/publications/decade/decade33/pages/gaza1.aspx.

4 On 2012–13 see: The Washington Post, November 13, 2013, http://www.washingtonpost.com/world/middle_east/a-year-after-war-gaza-israel-front-is-calm/2013/11/13/cb963f0e-4bb6-11e3-bf60-c1ca136ae14a_story.html.

5 *The Algemeiner*, March 13, 2014, http://www.algemeiner.com/2014/03/13/israeli-ministers-say-retaking-gaza-is-only-way-to-stop-rockets/.

7 On the war of 2014 see: The New Face of Conflict, A Report by the JINSA-Commissioned Gaza Conflict Task Force, March 2015, http://www.jinsa.org/files/2014GazaAssessmentReport.pdf.

8 The Washington Institute for Near East Policy, July 30, 2014, http://www.washingtoninstitute.org/policy-analysis/view/how-to-think-about-the-new-middle-east.

9 *The Times*, April 5, 2013, http://www.thetimes.co.uk/tto/news/world/middleeast/article3731407.ece.

10 Brookings, November 21, 2013, http://www.brookings.edu/blogs/iran-at-saban/posts/2013/11/21-iran-terrorism-problem-beirut-bombing-byman.

11 On the "Karine A" see: Amos Harel, and Avi Isacharoff, *The Seventh War* (Tel Aviv: Miskal: Yedioth Ahronoth Books and Chemed Books, 2004), 180.

12 Yoaz Hendel, and Yaakov Katz, *Israel vs. Iran: The Shadow War* (Dulles: Virginia Potomac Books, 2012), 25.

13 On the effect of the 2006 war see: Matthew Levitt, *Hezbollah: The Global Footprint of Lebanon's Party of God* (Georgetown University Press, 2013), 5.

14 On cutting aid see: The Telegraph, May 31, 2013, http://www.telegraph.co.uk/news/worldnews/middleeast/palestinianauthority/10091629/Iran-cuts-Hamas-funding-over-Syria.html.

15 *The Washington Post*, July 14, 2014, https://www.washingtonpost.com/world/middle_east/israel-shoots-down-hamas-drone/2014/07/14/991c46da-0b47-11e4-b8e5-d0de80767fc2_story.html.

16 *Jerusalem Post*, May 18, 2016.

17 *Jerusalem Post*, May 19, 2015, http://www.jpost.com/Opinion/The-next-Gaza-war-that-nobody-wants-403563.

18 BBC, September 1, 2014, http://www.bbc.com/news/world-middle-east-28439404. United Nations Office for the Coordination of

Humanitarian Affairs, January 27-9, 2009, http://www.ochaopt.org/documents/ocha_opt_gaza_humanitarian_situation_report_2009_01_29_english.pdf.

19 Reuters, June 2, 2014, http://www.reuters.com/article/2014/06/02/us-palestinian-unity-divisions-idUSKBN0ED1DX20140602.

20 The Washington Institute for Near East Policy, September 2010, http://www.washingtoninstitute.org/policy-analysis/view/if-war-comes-israel-vs.-hizballah-and-its-allies.

21 *Jerusalem Post*, April 18, 2016, http://www.jpost.com/Arab-Israeli-Conflict/IDF-uncovers-Hamas-tunnel-stretching-from-Gaza-into-Israel-451556.

22 Report of the detailed findings of the independent commission of inquiry established pursuant to Human Rights Council resolution S-21/1. June 22, 2015, p. 183.

23 Haaretz, January 4, 2013, http://www.haaretz.co.il/news/politics/1.1900172.

24 Al Monitor, February 15, 2013, http://www.al-monitor.com/pulse/originals/2013/02/siton-shamir-the-jordanian-option-isnt-an-option.html.

25 *Jerusalem Post*, July 11, 2013, http://www.jpost.com/Middle-East/Kerry-extends-its-stay-in-Mideast-says-significant-progress-made-in-some-areas-of-peace-talks-330912.

26 Ynet, January 2, 2014, http://www.ynet.co.il/articles/0,7340,L-4472168,00.html.

27 Al Monitor, January 10, 2014, http://www.al-monitor.com/pulse/en/originals/2014/01/third-intifada-settlers-hilltop-youth-price-tag-terror.html.

28 Al Monitor, May 19, 2014, http://www.al-monitor.com/pulse/en/originals/2014/05/palestine-israel-journalism-intifada-avi-issacharoff-attack.html.

29 Brookings, June 8, 2014, http://www.brookings.edu/blogs/up-front/posts/2014/06/08-palestine-national-movement-elgindy.

30 *The Guardian*, July 4, 2014, http://www.theguardian.com/commentisfree/2014/jul/04/vengeance-third-intifada-killing-israeli-palestinian.

31 Israel's channel 2, July 3, 2014, http://reshet.tv/%D7%97%D7%93%D7%A9%D7%95%D7%AA/News/Opinion/Article,156073.aspx.

32 *The Washington Post*, November 19, 2014, http://www.washingtonpost.com/opinions/israeli-and-palestinian-leaders-know-what-they-need-to-do-to-stop-a-third-intifada/2014/11/19/20d12a30-7026-11e4-ad12-3734c461eab6_story.html.

33 Brookings, January 29, 2015, http://www.brookings.edu/~/media/Research/Files/Papers/2015/01/29%20israel%20middle%20east%20rabinovich/Israel%20Rabinovich%2001292015.pdf.

34 Besa Center, April 13, 2015, http://besacenter.org/perspectives-papers/the-middle-east-turmoil-and-israels-security/.

35 Clingendael report, April 2015, http://www.clingendael.nl/publication/adversity-and-opportunity.

36 CFR, July 2015, http://www.cfr.org/palestine/violent-uprising-west-bank/p36842.

37 *Jerusalem Post*, September 7, 2015, http://www.jpost.com/Jerusalem-Report/A-third-intifada-or-a-political-process-415148.

38 *The Times of Israel*, October 4, 2015, http://www.timesofisrael.com/a-personal-intifada-not-a-mass-uprising/.

39 Center for Strategic International Studies (CSIS), November 10, 2015, http://csis.org/publication/israel-and-palestinians-issues-obama-netanyahu-meeting-failed-address.

40 Al Monitor, January 8, 2016, http://www.al-monitor.com/pulse/en/originals/2016/01/israel-mofaz-interview-violence-intifada-diplomatic-plan.html#.

41 *The Times of Israel*, February 7, 2016, http://www.timesofisrael.com/poll-support-for-third-intifada-waning-among-palestinians/.

42 Al Monitor, March 14, 2016, http://www.al-monitor.com/pulse/originals/2016/03/israel-palestine-third-intifada-failure-no-leadership-chaos.html.

43 On that fight see: Zeev Schiff, and Ehud Ya'ari, *Intifada* (Tel Aviv: Schocken, 1990).

44 Al Monitor, January 31, 2014, http://www.al-monitor.com/pulse/originals/2014/01/al-qaeda-israel-threat.html#.

45 Al Monitor, May 16, 2014, http://www.al-monitor.com/pulse/iw/originals/2014/05/west-bank-demonstrations-crossing-point-security-cooperation.html.

46 Ynet, June 2, 2014, http://www.ynet.co.il/articles/0,7340,L-4526295,00.html.

47 On the number see: Ynet, March 23, 2015, http://www.ynet.co.il/articles/0,7340,L-4640070,00.html.

Chapter 5

A Future Clash between Israel and Egypt

Israel has been eager to keep the peace with Egypt, and it seems Egypt ruled by Al-Sisi is on the same page with Israel in this matter. However, subsequent to the unrest in Egypt since 2011, trouble may brew in several spots, causing tension that might even end with a clash between the two states. The danger of such an occurrence stems from Egypt's economic troubles and the low-intensity war in Sinai.

Diverting attention toward Israel

Some assume that the lack of democracy in the Arab world is a result of its societies not being ready for it, due to their culture and religion. Another view blames the United States for supporting authoritarian leaders in order to protect Israel and/or secure the flow of oil and block Iran and radical Islam.[1] In Egypt, the United States tolerated Hosni Mubarak's dictatorship (1981–2011) because he kept the peace with Israel, allowed American aircraft and ships to cross his country, and opposed Islamic extremists, both Sunni ones like Al Qaeda and Shi'ite ones such as Iran.

Anthony Cordesman stated in March 2014, "It now seems all too likely that it will take at least half a decade for Egypt to find a new balance between military rule and a more open political system that will create lasting political consensus and stability."[2] Jonathan Spyer claimed in early May 2014 that the regime in Egypt "is likely to combine authoritarian and representative elements, accompanied by a smoldering Islamist attempt at insurgency. It will, however, conclusively draw a line under the possibility of the emergence of a Sunni Iran on the Nile," which would get Egypt support from Israel and Saudi Arabia.[3] Yet Robert Kagan, a senior fellow at the Brookings Institution, warned in April 2014 that although Israel supports the current Egyptian government, the latter might turn against Israel, "playing to public opinion."[4] In 2013, there were already signs that Arab states might try to divert internal pressures outside, against Israel.[5] In this sense in 2015, Egypt's economy continued to struggle such as with getting foreign investments.[6] In February 2016, Jon Alterman presented a grim picture of Egypt's economy.[7] If a major economic crisis erupts and gets out of control, it may tempt the Egyptian government to seek an outlet for public rage by directing it toward Israel. A clash with Israel may not necessarily be the intention of this move, but it could bring about such a result.

Since 2011 the Egyptian military has occasionally collaborated with every major political faction inside Egypt; nevertheless, it could still find itself opposed to a vast coalition of its former partners. The Egyptian military—if strongly pressured by the public to give up some of its economic and political privileges—might then strive for a very limited clash with Israel, aiming to prove its worth to the homeland on the battlefield.

Unrest and civil war in Egypt

Egypt's national cohesiveness and stability are based on its long, rich, and famous history as a state and on the fact that almost all its population is Arab and Sunni. Other Arab states that don't share those characteristics, like Libya, Syria, and Iraq, have been suffering from unrest bordering on a civil war. However, Egypt has its own major internal hardships, which erupted in 2011 and have been seething ever since, due to economic, political, ideological, and religious problems.

In the 1990s, there was a fierce struggle between the Mubarak regime and radical Islamists.[8] In 2013–2014, there were talks about a possible civil war in Egypt.[9] Following their fall from power in

July 2013, the Muslim Brotherhood (MB) or some of its members might collaborate with Salafis and other Egyptian groups, more secular ones, such as those that had started the revolution but fear the current regime. If the latter faces unrest and growing resistance, including a violent one, and is pushed to take drastic steps, turning the country against Israel might be one of them.

Sahar Aziz, an associate professor of law at Texas A&M School of Law, claimed that in Egypt "the military and internal security forces had been trained for over 60 years to view Islamists, whether the nonviolent MB or their more extremist jihadi counterparts, with deep suspicion."[11] Yet Hillel Frisch, a senior research associate at the Begin-Sadat Center for Strategic Studies, mentioned in 2013 that it must be assumed that in Egypt "at least half of the army recruits are supporters of the MB and Salafis."[12] If there is a civil war, Egyptian troops might desert and some might also join radical Islamic groups. If the latter gradually have the upper hand, the Egyptian government, as a last resort, might increase the rhetoric against Israel in a desperate attempt to deflect the blame and gain support. Another possibility is that the regime might reach a deal with its foes at the expense of Israel.

According to Zack Gold, in 2013, "given the broad opposition to Israel in Egyptian society, it is fair to presume that many soldiers and officers share these views personally." Also, "both Egyptian Islamists and secular nationalists generally oppose aspects, if not the entirety, of the Egyptian–Israeli relationship. Islamists already have significant credibility with the public on the issue; it is the secular nationalist camp that tends to be more vocal in its opposition."[13] In November 2015, a large numbers of Egyptians saw Israel as an enemy.[14] This anti-Israeli approach might contribute to the willingness of many Egyptians to direct their efforts against Israel rather than fight among themselves.

The challenges in Sinai

Egypt made attempts to develop the Sinai but failed, owing to more urgent priorities,[15] and the fact is that almost the entire Egyptian population and most of their civilian and military infrastructure is situated outside Sinai, west of the Suez Canal. From Egypt's strategic perspective, the Sinai is primarily a defense zone in time of war against Israel in case the Israel Defense Forces (IDF) invades. Egypt views abolishing the demilitarization of Sinai, one of the conditions of the peace agreement between Egypt and Israel, as a long overdue necessity that must be addressed, and defending Egyptian sovereignty in Sinai could be used as an excuse to send many troops over there. The population in the peninsula, about half a million, might be exploited for this purpose as well. Egypt might claim that it must deploy its military all over Sinai in order to protect its population, without mentioning of course that Egypt has neglected them for decades.

In recent years, the Sinai has been lawless and a battlefield of low-intensity war between the Egyptian government and guerrilla and terror groups.[16] The latter launched many assaults, some quite deadly. On August 5, 2012, near the border between Israel and Egypt, 16 Egyptian border guards were killed in a surprise attack. On August 19, 2013, in an ambush in northeast Sinai, 25 Egyptian troops were killed, some of them literally executed. On July 1, 2015, in a series of clashes in Sinai, 17 Egyptian troops were killed.

Egypt has launched several operations in Sinai in recent years. Restoring security was essential for bringing back tourists, an important industry in the peninsula. Suppressing the guerrilla and terror groups also required financial investments in creating infrastructure and jobs for the Bedouin population in the peninsula. This was needed in order to reduce their motivation to collaborate with guerrilla and terror groups . Such a policy has been quite expensive, and Egypt, with its huge economic challenges, has found it very difficult to allocate budgets for those projects.

The armed groups in Sinai are a security problem for Israel too, which explains Israel's repeated consent to reinforce Egypt's deployment in the Sinai as part of the fight against guerrilla and terror groups there. In May 2014, in Sinai there were two Egyptian infantry brigades, one tank battalion and a squadron of AH-64 gunships. Every few months Israel renews its permission that allows those units to stay in the peninsula.[17] Israel has been willing to tolerate the increased Egyptian military presence across Sinai, but up to a certain point. If Egypt stresses the need to deploy many more forces in the peninsula, Israel might suspect that Egypt is exploiting the chaos in Sinai to slowly end the demilitarization. Israel might turn down the Egyptian demand, which could create a high level of tension between the two states.

Additional Egyptian forces might not guarantee quiet if they are not used properly. They might be ineffective due to a misguided strategy such as a heavy-handed approach. David Schenker, director of a program on Arab politics at the Washington Institute, describes such a case.[18] In mid-2015, the Egyptian military's "poor tactics and morale" contributed to the failure in suppressing the insurgents in the peninsula.[19]

Eric Trager, an expert on Egyptian politics at the Washington Institute, mentioned in mid-May 2015 that "the Sisi era has also witnessed unprecedented coordination between Israel and Egypt on counterterrorism in the Sinai."[20] The coordination between Israel and Egypt has improved since Morsi's government was toppled in July 2013. When Morsi was in power, his movement, the MB, was not quite "brothers in arms" of Israel in its struggle against guerrilla and terror groups in Sinai, although the MB looked for calm there too. It's possible that the MB, being a radical Islamic movement like many of the groups in Sinai, could have found nonviolent ways to deal with them, but it's doubtful that an understanding could have been reached, particularly with those groups associated with Al Qaeda.

Bruce Maddy-Weitzman is a professor in the Department of Middle Eastern and African History in Tel Aviv University. He said on March 7, 2016, that in spite of security cooperation between Israel and Egypt, their relationship would be harmed because of "socio-cultural and political–ideological factors that touch on the fundamental core identity and self-image of the Egyptian polity."[21]

Israel finished its withdrawal from Sinai in the early 1980s, following the peace treaty, and did not invade it again. But Israel also had a peace accord with the PA, which did not prevent the IDF from recapturing in 2002 area A in the West Bank, a zone that was under direct control of the PA.

Steven A. Cook is the Hasib J. Sabbagh Senior Fellow for Middle Eastern Studies at the Council on Foreign Relations. He warned that following the fight inside Sinai, an assault from there by insurgents that would cause Israel many casualties could bring an Israeli response, "potentially compromising the Egypt–Israel peace treaty."[22]

In early July 2016, a former senior Israeli official claimed that Israel had launched several drone strikes in Sinai in recent years.[23] One or a series of deadly terrorist attacks against Israel from Sinai might bring Israel to urge Egypt to allow the IDF to be more involved in fighting guerrilla and terror groups in the peninsula. Israel has much more experience in this field than Egypt. Israel might even demand to do the job alone. Although Israel has been collaborating with Egypt in this matter, Israel might decide, as it was with the PA in 2002, that in Sinai too its Arab partner is not willing to and/or not capable of helping Israel maintain security. Israel might ask Egypt to penetrate into Sinai temporarily for a major air and/or ground operation. Egypt, solely for political reasons, would probably strongly oppose such an Israeli action. This might cause a serious crisis between the two states.

The Suez Canal is another sensitive area within Egyptian jurisdiction. According to Cook, both Egyptian and U.S. officials regard the potential for terrorists to disrupt the functioning of the Canal a "low probability."[24] Yet, particularly following the fluid situation in Egypt, if the latter seems unable to secure the Suez Canal, Western states might consider eventually taking action, including militarily, despite Egypt's will. The Western aim would probably be to avoid clashes with the Egyptian military, but they could happen anyway. At the same time, Israel might exploit this opportunity to run its own campaign against guerrilla and terror groups in east Sinai. Israel might coordinate its steps with Western states in a covert way so it would not look like a Western–Israeli offensive against Egypt. There might be some similarity to the 1956 war, when Israel, Britain, and France signed a secret agreement and attacked Egypt. In 1956, Britain and France wanted to gain control of the Suez Canal while Israel was focused on Sinai. As it was then, a repetition of such a move in the future might also turn out to be a dangerous adventure.

Egypt and the PA

In late November 2014, Al-Sisi suggested that after a Palestinian state is established, Egypt can assist in stabilizing it, including by deploying Egyptian forces there.[25] If there is eventually a Palestinian state, the Israeli–Palestinian conflict might continue, particularly if the Palestinians declare a state without signing an agreement with Israel. Even if Israel accepts the new Palestinian state, there might be friction and even violence between Israel and the Palestinian government and/or Palestinian groups. If there are indeed Egyptian forces inside the Palestinian state, Israel would have to avoid striking Palestinian areas where Egyptian forces would be deployed. Palestinians who would attack Israel might hide near Egyptian troops. If Israel, by accident, harms Egyptian troops, as part of an attempt to hit Palestinians who fight against Israel, there might be a rift between Israel and Egypt. This crisis might escalate if Egyptian forces in Palestinian territory fire back and the IDF does the same. Egypt's government, even against its will, due to public pressure, might have to act against Israel. Sending reinforcements to the Palestinian state without Israeli approval would worsen the crisis. Egypt could dispatch troops to the West Bank only through Jordan, which might refuse to allow that because it would violate Jordan's peace treaty with Israel. Even if

Jordan agrees, if Egyptian units seek to enter the West Bank, it would mean confronting the IDF.

On July 21, 2016, Al-Sisi said that his country's effort to restart the talks between Israel and the Palestinians should "make everyone face their responsibilities." He warned "of the consequences of delays in achieving peace."[26] If there is no peace agreement, let alone if there is another confrontation between Israel and the Palestinians in the West Bank, then Egypt could blame Israel, which would increase the tension between the two countries.

The nuclear factor

After the war against Iraq in 1991, Egypt claimed that restraint of Iraq rendered Israel's need for nuclear weapons redundant.[27] If Iran is completely prevented, one way or another, from producing a Bomb, Egypt might argue again that Israel does not require such an arsenal. This issue has been a bone of contention between Israel and Egypt for many years and could cause a crisis at a certain point. This alone would not ignite a clash, but together with other factors it might.

Egypt halted its own nuclear project in the 1970s.[28] In January 2007, Mubarak raised the possibility of his country aspiring to gain nuclear weapons as a response to Iran's effort in this field.[29] In February 2015, Russia and Egypt declared that they were going to build a nuclear reactor in Egypt together.[30] Egypt's severe economic problems would prevent it from investing heavily in a nuclear program. If Iran produces a Bomb, Egypt might try to build one too, together with other Arab states, mostly those near Iran. This would be the Arab Sunni Bomb. Another option, more likely, is that Saudi Arabia buys and controls its own nuclear weapon that might protect Egypt too. The latter, for its part, might promise to dispatch its conventional forces, the strongest ones in the Arab world, to help Saudi Arabia in a war against Iran.[31] The Saudi and Egyptian militaries trained together and collaborated with each other in the war in Yemen in 2015. If their conventional option fails, they would have a nuclear one as backup. Such a strategy would be against Iran, but it might raise the tension between Israel and Arab states, including Egypt.

Egypt kept the peace with Israel after Israeli raids on Arab nuclear sites in 1981 (Iraq) and 2007 (Syria), since it served Egypt's interests. Egypt was opposed to Syria and Iraq possessing the Bomb. Post-Mubarak, Egypt would not want Iran to acquire a nuclear weapon. However, if a confrontation between Iran and Israel occurred, and the relationship between the latter and Egypt was at a low point, Egypt might take advantage of Israel's war with Iran to nullify the demilitarization of the Sinai and send in tens of thousands of troops. Israel might tolerate that in order not to become entangled in a double-front war, with Iran in the east and Egypt in the southwest. When the war with Iran ended, Israel would seek to drive Egyptian forces out of Sinai, but that would risk a collision between the two countries.

IDF's buildup

In 1991, the anti-Iraqi coalition—well trained in high-intensity warfare as the American forces were—won the battles. In a future war, if the IDF starts a massive ground attack in Sinai, its units also have to be ready to beat their foe in a high-intensity war. If the IDF is well prepared for a war against Egypt, the latter might be deterred, which might prevent a confrontation.

There could be a high-intensity war between Israel and Egypt.[32] The militaries of Egypt and Israel lack experience in this kind of combat. The last time Israel had such a confrontation was in 1982 against Syrian forces in Lebanon, and Egypt had it in 1991 against Iraq. The Egyptian military has been training for the last 30 years for high-intensity war against the IDF, while the latter had to fight and train for a hybrid and low-intensity war in that period. Although the IDF also trained for a high-intensity war against Syria, it was against a different enemy and in a terrain different from what was expected in Sinai. The Israeli drills for a strike in

Iran largely distract the Israeli Air Force (IAF) from training for missions on the Egyptian front, like storming airfields.

In 2015, the IDF had 465,000 reserve troops.[33] The IDF needs a division or more with expertise in desert warfare in a high-intensity war. This brings to mind the famous "Desert Rats," the British 7th Armored Division in North Africa during the Second World War. The IDF has also the "Givati" brigade, an infantry unit that is very familiar with the south of Israel, the Negev, which is similar to Sinai, and could be trained to deal with the Egyptian military. The symbol of this brigade is the fox. The desert fox is well known as an inspiration for daring maneuvers in the desert. German commander Ervin Rommel was thus nicknamed owing to his worldwide reputation in desert warfare. On several occasions the tactics of the IDF were compared to his.[34] It should be imperative for the IDF to have units ready to deal specifically with the Egyptian military.

Considering the might of the Egyptian military and the challenges of high-intensity warfare in Sinai, the IDF needs to conduct many drills including large-scale ones. As it is extremely expensive to run major exercises, particularly corps level, the IDF has to rely on limited drills, for instance, when a battalion represents a brigade or when only officers and noncommissioned officers participate in the training.

The Egyptian military might surprise the IDF as it did in February 1960, when Egypt suddenly reinforced its units in Sinai and Israel received no alert.[35] It might occur again although the odds of that happening don't seem to be high, considering the capabilities of Israeli intelligence. The ongoing transferring of many Israeli units, including from the intelligence community, to camps in the Negev in the upcoming years might help in this matter. Early notice is essential for the IDF because it depends on the reserves, which require a few days to mobilize and get organized.

In recent years, the IAF has made changes to improve its bombing capabilities. There were major changes in the IDF buildup in favor of the air force, intelligence, and elite infantry at the expense of the armor. In a future war, even if the IAF achieves air superiority and inflicts substantial blows to Egyptian ground units in Sinai, it might not be enough to kick all the Egyptian forces out of their positions in the peninsula. Completing this task might require an Israeli land offensive. Its success would depend on the readiness of Israeli ground units. This means training the armor, infantry, artillery, combat engineers, logistics, and ordnance.

The IDF's chief of general staff, Lt. General Gadi Eizenkot, emphasizes training and readiness. Nevertheless, in its exercises the IDF focuses on hybrid foes like Hamas and Hezbollah. A collision with the Egyptian armed forces might show that the IDF is not fully ready for a high-intensity war. This outcome might have grave consequences. Obviously, on-the-job training would not be the best solution, to put it mildly. The Egyptian military was defeated in less than a week in 1956 and in 3 days in 1967, but this was done after years of preparations for such a demanding mission.

Egyptian buildup

Between October 11 and November 6, 2014, Egypt ran the Bader-2014 exercise, its biggest drill since 1996, which was meant to examine, among others, a scenario of a war with Israel.[36] It showed that at least part of the Egyptian military kept on training in spite of the economic crisis in its country, and one of the purposes was to prepare for a possible war against Israel.

In 2015, Egypt's military had 479,000 reserve troops. "The Egyptian military remained far too focused on quantity versus quality with an unwieldy military structure."[37] However, "for all its inherent weaknesses, the Egyptian military will maintain its considerable strength in conventional warfare. It is undeniably well equipped and, in some ways, well trained for conventional battles, and it has increasingly benefitted from the acquisition of sophisticated modern weaponry and joint training exercises with advanced foreign militaries, such as that of the United States ... However, it will be at a clear disadvantage against Israel's rapid and flexible troops."[38] In a war against the IDF, the Egyptian military might be inferior in some areas, mostly in the air, but its men might put up a tough fight on land.

Near the end of the 1973 war, Henry Kissinger, U.S. secretary of state, emphasized that he did not see any estimate before the war indicating that the Arabs could beat the IDF or even avoid defeat for more than six days.[39] In the future it would be careless to underestimate the Egyptian military, which has some operational capabilities and whose troops are familiar with the battlefield in Sinai, where they had trained and even fought in recent years.

In 1967, the Egyptian military had 11 years both to recover from its defeat in 1956 and to prepare for another war. The 1967 war proved that those efforts were insufficient and did not prevent an Egyptian catastrophe. A future war would show if the Egyptian military has used recent decades to get ready for a high-intensity war.

According to Aram Nerguizian in 2015, Egypt's air force had "capable aircrew, good aircraft serviceability, and high standards of maintenance." Furthermore, "Israel remained uneasy with Egypt's efforts to acquire offensive naval systems. Meanwhile, Egypt continued to view Israeli concerns surrounding its military edge as a persistent impediment to Egyptian military development efforts."[40] It is quite difficult for both states to reach a compromise on this issue.

In the 1950s, Egypt's military made a drastic shift in its buildup when it changed from depending on a Western arsenal, the British one, to Soviet weapons. Egypt did this kind of turn again in the late 1970s, when it came back to rely once again on Western weapon systems, this time mostly American ones, which included assimilating >200 F-16s and about a thousand M1A1 tanks.

Over the years the United States argued that Arab states, having armed themselves with American weapons, became "too dependent on U.S. training, spare parts, and support to be in a position to use sophisticated U.S.-made arms against" Israel.[41] The United States has supplied the Egyptian military with thousands of weapon systems since the late 1970s. If Egypt collides with Israel, the United States might immediately cut all its aid to Egypt. Yet the latter might continue fighting for at least a few weeks by implementing steps like the cannibalization of its weapon systems[42] and then replacing what was lost in combat with a Russian arsenal. Egypt could also adopt strategies like prolonging or slowing down the war in order to deal with a shortage of spare parts and ammunition.

In a future war, there would be identification problems because both sides have American weapon systems like the M-113 APCs and the M-109 self-propelled guns. Each military might capture some of those vehicles but should avoid using them as is, with enemy marks on them, because this would increase the danger of friendly fire. A land unit mistakenly attacking a friendly force might be somewhat traumatized and hesitate too much the next time when it is not clear whom they are encountering. On the other hand, troops who waited too long to make sure, and then experienced the bitter surprise of encountering a foe who fired first, might be overaggressive the next time they run into an unrecognized force. Those two negative approaches, firing too fast or too late, might become more and more common as the campaign continues. Sooner or later most soldiers could be involved directly or indirectly in some kind of friendly fire.

Israel and high- and low-intensity wars

"A military that retains both joint combined-arms fire and maneuver capabilities, as well as the flexibility and population focus of a counterinsurgency campaign, will have the requisite tools to succeed against a hybrid adversary."[43] The 2006 war in Lebanon showed the lack of readiness of the IDF for hybrid warfare, after years of fighting only low-intensity war, while neglecting both hybrid and high-intensity warfare.

Following the tension between Israel and Syria after the collapse of the peace talks between them in 2008,[44] the IDF had to increase its investment not only in preparing for another round against the Hezbollah but also for a possible high-intensity war against Syria. Since then the IDF has trained mostly against three foes: the Hezbollah, another hybrid force; the Hamas in the Gaza Strip; and a conventional military, the Syrian one. There was also the probability of a major Israeli air raid on Iran that could have generated a war, keeping the IAF busy with this task as well.

Israel's overall preparations for various wars contributed in a way to the readiness of the IDF for a possible high-intensity war against Egypt. Yet, considering the unique conditions of the Egyptian front, training for a high-intensity war against Syria, let alone against hybrid foes, was a distraction and sometimes counterproductive too. Even the combination of the Syrian military, the Hezbollah, and the Hamas is less powerful than the Egyptian military, another reason it might be a challenge for Israel to defeat it. Furthermore, in a future war against Egypt, the IDF might not get a month to adapt as in the 2006 war, but only a few days, a fact that requires Israel to be ready in advance for this front.

For Israeli soldiers, who have been used for many years now to dealing with guerrilla and terror groups in mostly urban and populated areas, the open area of Sinai would be a different theater of operation. It is also essential to train manpower, such as soldiers *in the armor*, in handling clashes between tanks, on a scale of several dozen up to a few hundred tanks. On the Syrian front, this kind of combat was much less likely in recent years. On other fronts like Lebanon and the Gaza Strip, it did not exist at all. As those fronts are the focus of the IDF, Israeli troops would not be ready to fight Egyptian armor if they were sent to Sinai by the Egyptian command. Israel's survival would not be at stake due to its nuclear weapons, but neglecting the possibility of a high-intensity war against the Egyptian military might cost Israel dearly.

One of the Israeli lessons from the 1973 and the 2006 wars was not to rely too much on a certain military concept. In 1973, the IDF thought that the war would be a fast and easy win, just like it was in the Six Day War in 1967. In 2006, the IDF believed that it would be more or less like the confrontation with the Palestinians in 2000–2005, i.e., with a foe that was not that strong. However, it did not turn out that way in either 1973 or 2006. A similar assumption could become a blunder again if the IDF estimates that the Israeli success in its encounters with the Hamas in recent years, such as in 2014, would repeat itself in a campaign against the Egyptian military.

In the war of 2006, Israel had to protect its population while reducing the risk to its soldiers in Lebanon to the minimum. The Egyptian military might not hit Israeli civilian targets as a barrage of rockets during a hybrid war would do. However, the IDF's casualties in Sinai might be much higher than the 119 dead soldiers the IDF suffered in Lebanon in 2006. This could happen due to the capabilities and firepower of the Egyptian military, which are more deadly than those of the Hezbollah.

In recent years, Israel has built a fence on the border with Egypt against illegal immigrants from Sudan, Eritrea, and other African countries who slip through Egypt into Israel. This measure proved successful, but it would not necessarily stop guerrilla and terror groups, who are still capable of penetrating Israel. They could also launch rockets, firing above the fence. Furthermore, the fence is the only artificial obstacle that separates the most powerful Arab military and Israel. Not much to depend on in case of a high-intensity war. The traditional Israeli approach in such matters was not to build expensive fortifications but to rely on attack if an Arab military invades Israel.

The IDF should consider the Egyptian front as a potential battlefield of a high-intensity war, not only as a theater where there might be a low intensity/hybrid war against armed groups in Sinai. In the mid-1950s, the border war between Israel and Egypt, which was a low-intensity war zone, ended up being an area of high-intensity war in 1956. A larger scale low-intensity war, the war of attrition in 1967–1970 between Israel and Egypt, was another stage on the road to the high-intensity war in 1973. In the future the current low-intensity war in Sinai might entangle Israel and Egypt against each other in skirmishes like those in the 1950s and in the worst case like the hostilities in 1967–1970.

Israel has been tolerating the Hezbollah with its 150,000 rockets. However, Israel prevented the Hezbollah in recent years from receiving advanced weapons from Assad, and Israel could eventually attack Iran, particularly if the latter is about to produce nuclear weapons. This means Israel does have its red lines and it might take military measures in case of a mass Egyptian deployment in Sinai.

Some assume there will not be any more wars between states or in the few times those wars occur, they will create a vacuum where nonstate organizations "would thrive."[45] If Israel inflicts a serious blow on Egypt in a future war, it might worsen the already shaky situation in Egypt. Parts of the latter, particularly Sinai, might become more lawless than they are now. Armed groups might pour into Egypt and turn it into their base, as in Syria.

During the past decades, the IDF had to fight again and again in hybrid or low-intensity wars, not in a high-intensity war. It would not be easy for Israeli troops to switch and quickly adjust to high-intensity warfare, considering the demands of such a confrontation and the strength of an Arab conventional military compared with any foe in a hybrid or low-intensity war. The 2006 war proved that the IDF had difficulties in changing its patterns and mentality from handling low-intensity war in the West Bank and the Gaza Strip to facing a hybrid enemy in Lebanon. If the rival in 2006 had been an Arab military, the ramifications for the IDF might have been even worse.

Following the meltdown of Syria and its military, Israel's main challenge in a possible high-intensity war is Jordan and/or Egypt, as unexpected as it might seem. In a very bad scenario for Israel, there might be a severe crisis and even a collision between Israel and Egypt during a war between Israel and Iran or the Hezbollah. The IDF would have to split its units to face the strongest Arab military on one front and deal with the strongest Arab nonstate organization and one of the most powerful non-Arab states in the Middle East on other fronts.

The United States, Egypt, Israel and high- and low-intensity wars

The U.S. military has been trying to convince Egypt's top brass not to prepare anymore for "bygone wars and spend more American money on border security, as well as counterterrorism and surveillance equipment and training that a truly modern military needs."[46] Derek Chollet, assistant secretary of defense for International Security Affairs, said on October 29, 2013, that the United States wants "Egypt to develop a military that is prepared to meet the threats of the twenty-first century."[47] But from the Egyptian perspective, it seems that the United States might have urged Egypt to conduct this reform in order to exploit Egyptian troops in fighting guerrilla and terror groups around the Middle East. Egypt, after it was burned in its low-intensity war in Yemen in the 1960s, does not want to repeat this adventure, certainly not by serving the United States. In 1967, Egypt absorbed its biggest military defeat in modern times, among others because a large number of Egyptian troops were stuck in Yemen when the 1967 war started. This is the essence of the dispute. As seen in the past decades, Egypt believes that its military should focus on a possible high-intensity war against Israel, not on counterinsurgency in Muslim countries. Yet if the ongoing low-intensity war in Sinai sufficiently concerns the Egyptian military, its high command might conclude that a major turn in doctrine and buildup is required.

The Egyptian military rejected the idea of stopping the production of tanks, partly because a joint U.S.–Egyptian co-production of tanks meant jobs for Egyptians.[48] Yet Egypt could give up many of its weapon systems like tanks and aircraft because they are not needed in huge numbers to handle a low-intensity war. By making such a drastic shift, Egypt would also save money, which is essential due to its deep economic crisis. The Egyptian military might agree if it keeps its strength, including political and economic advantages, along with its prestige as defender of the state.

On October 9, 2013, the Obama administration announced that it was "recalibrating our assistance to Egypt to best advance our interests."[49] The United States withheld part of the military aid to Egypt. This meant a delay in sending major weapon systems, such as F-16s, AH-64s, and M1A1s, while continuing the support in aspects such as the counterinsurgency program and securing Sinai.[50] According to Eric Trager, the result of this move was that "the administration will reinforce the perception in Egypt that the military aid's primary goal is to keep Israel safe, and that Washington does not care about Egyptians' well-being."[51]

Egypt's perspective could be that the F-16s and M1A1s are supposed to defend their country, which means allowing it to fight a high-intensity war against Israel. The latter would rather divert Egypt from concentrating on a high-intensity war against it while directing Egypt to crush armed groups in Sinai that pose a threat to Egypt and Israel as well. Israel wants Egypt to be secured so foreign investments and tourism, which forms one of Egypt's major revenues, are revived, thus helping to stabilize Egypt. For the Obama administration, this goal, "desirable in principle, is a second-tier priority," says Michael O'Hanlon, a senior fellow, and Jeremy Shapiro, a fellow, both from the Brookings Institute.[52] Stability in Egypt is essential to keeping its peace treaty with Israel, a top priority for the latter and a very important interest for the United States.

In late 2013, the Egyptian government complained about the United States supporting the MB. However, America assisted the

Egyptian military in counterinsurgency, i.e., fighting those in the MB who chose violence after their president, Morsi, was removed from power and their movement became an enemy of the state. The United States and Egypt, in spite of all their disputes, have agreed that Egypt's enemy was internal. The military aid was the best leverage the United States had in persuading Egypt that its most vital national security interest is learning how to run a low-intensity war, with as little collateral damage as possible. The need for the United States, Israel, and Egypt to change Egypt's approach made it seem to the Obama administration worth taking certain risks, such as sending signals about adjusting the American aid to Egypt.

The cut in the aid to Egypt was announced on October 9, 2013, a few days after Egypt celebrated what it considers its victory—the 1973 Ramadan war against Israel. More than 50 Egyptians were killed during the marking of that event, due to clashes between Islamists and their rivals.[53] In a kind of symbolic linkage, the Obama administration reminded Egypt that the 1973 confrontation must remain the last high-intensity war between Israel and Egypt, particularly because the latter had other national security challenges, for instance, enforcing law and order while avoiding harming civilians.

Israel commemorated 40 years since the 1973 Yom Kippur War by returning to the battles in Sinai and debating why and how things went wrong and what lessons should have been learned. In 2013 and ever since the 1973 war, the only combat that Israel wished to see in Sinai was between the Egyptian military and guerrilla and terror groups there.

Israel did not want to think about sending its AH-64 to destroy Egyptian armor in the peninsula but rather to watch Egypt's AH-64 hunting down insurgents in Sinai. In that sense "routine maintenance schedules typically ground more than a third" of Egypt's AH-64.[54] In July 2014, 12 out of 34 of Egypt's attack helicopters were not operational due to logistic reasons.[55] The AH-64 might be important not only in low-intensity war in Sinai. Those gunships are effective against both armed groups and Israeli ground forces, particularly because the latter are not used to dealing with this kind of threat.

In March 2015, the American aid was restored.[56] Israel, to begin with, opposed the cut in the American aid to Egypt, worrying about consequences to the peace treaty. In the U.S. congress some shared this concern.[57] For both Egypt and Israel, the American military aid to Egypt is part of the 1979 peace treaty, so reducing the aid might have allowed Egypt to ignore the rest of the accord. There were already voices in Egypt, calling to annul the treaty, particularly in recent years. Preventing the delivery of weapons to Egypt gave those who opposed the peace political ammunition.

On the other hand, Israel supported delivering Egypt weapon systems like the F-16, which is needed mostly for high-intensity war, i.e., against Israel. The Israeli concept was based on a dangerous paradox. If Israel wants peace with Egypt, the former should help prepare Egypt for high-intensity war, against Israel.

In recent years, the IDF has assumed that there might be a war with Egypt.[58] Yet such a collision, let alone a full-scale one, is probably the last scenario Israel wants to think about. Still, if this happens, Israel might assume it could beat the Egyptian military. Therefore, as to the American aid, if Egypt assimilates some more weapon systems like the F-16, it would not make much of a difference in the balance of power between Israel and Egypt.

Air war

In a time of war, both Israel and Egypt would strive to gain air superiority. The side that reached this goal would enjoy a decisive advantage, although a few of the remaining enemy fighter bombers and mostly gunships could still sneak in and cause casualties and damage.

Gaining air superiority could be done by wiping out enemy planes on the ground in their airfields or by conducting air-to-air battles.[59]

In 2014, the IAF allocated most of its budget to train in air-to-air combat,[60] a necessary investment in case of a war against Egypt. Yet the IAF has been focused on other fronts as well, in preparing to bomb the Iranian nuclear infrastructure and destroying rocket launchers in Lebanon as part of a campaign against the Hezbollah, as it was done in the campaign in the Gaza Strip in 2014.

The Israeli military industry invested in producing long-range air-to-air missiles, with a range of up to 100 kilometers. The Syrian air force is not much of a challenge for the IAF. Yet there are Arab states with advanced American aircraft that might confront the IAF. Egypt falls into that category too because it has >200 F-16s. In April 2015, Lt. Col. B, from the IAF, who is in charge of assimilating the F-35, argued that Egypt's air force is of the highest quality.[61] At that time Egypt bought 24 French Rafale jets, which caused Israel to wonder about Egypt's intentions.[62] In mid-February 2016, a senior Israeli defense official warned that Egypt purchased weapons as part of its focus on Israel. Hence, the latter must be ready for various scenarios and sharp shifts in the region.[63] He hinted that Egypt might become an enemy of Israel.

In the 1973 war and particularly in the 2006 war, the IDF put too much trust in its firepower, mostly that of the IAF. The latter did obtain important achievements in both wars, but they were insufficient as far as many in the IDF were concerned. It might be the same in a future war. If the war was solely between Israel and Egypt, the IAF could concentrate on Egypt, which was not feasible in 1973. On the other hand, the IAF might have to deal with all kinds of constraints and problems that did not exist in 1973 and 2006, harsh weather, for example. Under certain circumstances the IAF might also suffer from a shortage of ammunition. For example, there might be another war prior to the war with Egypt, such as against the Hezbollah and/or Iran, or there could be a delay of rearming by the United States due to deep disagreements within the American administration or a rift between the United States and Israel.

Egypt relied on antiaircraft batteries in the 1973 war. Those weapon systems, sometimes the same kind as in 1973, would still serve Egypt in a future war. In fact, many of Egypt's antiaircraft missile batteries are almost obsolete. Furthermore, the IAF is well aware of those weapons, following its experience and preparations for many years to fight Syria's antiaircraft batteries, many of which are similar to those of Egypt. It should also be noted that contrary to 1973, when the frontline was around the Suez Canal, in a future war Egyptian antiaircraft batteries would not be able to concentrate their firepower if they have to cover much more territory, all over Sinai.

In a future war, the IAF might be sent to bomb Egyptian infrastructure west of the Suez Canal in order to urge Egypt to leave Sinai. The latter could retaliate by launching long-range surface-to-surface missiles at Israeli cities. Egypt and Israel might strike only military targets because both states would be aware that bombardments of civilian areas would bring a fierce response and an escalation neither side would want.

The air war might run at sea as well. Egyptian planes, carrying anti-ship missiles like Harpoon, could jeopardize Israel's sea routes in the Mediterranean Sea. The IAF would have to intercept the Egyptian planes while protecting both civilian and military ships sometimes more than a thousand kilometers from Israel.

Offense and defense

If Egypt crosses the Rubicon, i.e., sends hundreds of tanks into the demilitarized areas in Sinai, Israel would probably seek to restore both the former status quo and its deterrence. This would mean inflicting a major blow to the Egyptian military, or at least threatening it with such a move, in order to drive the Egyptian military out of Sinai as soon as possible. Executing this plan would depend on the scale and location of the Egyptian forces in the peninsula.

In a future war, Egyptian troops would not possess fortified posts in most of Sinai. Without those strongholds, key spots might fall easily into the hands of the IDF, a move that could jeopardize the entire Egyptian grip on Sinai. Yet if the Egyptian military does not crumble early in the campaign, its troops might slow down the IDF's advance inside Sinai.

Due to political reasons, Egyptian forces would probably try to stop the IDF as close as possible to the border by relying on forward defense. Yet if Egyptian forces stay in west Sinai, relatively close to the Suez Canal, i.e., to their bases and airfields, it would be more difficult for the IDF to defeat them. The IDF might hesitate to advance all the way to the Suez Canal because of logistical, operational, and political constraints. The IDF might prefer a large Egyptian force advancing to northeast Sinai, in proximity to the IDF's camps, particularly airfields in the Negev. This would enable the IDF to bomb its foe like Egypt's lines of communications. If the Egyptian deployment is done in haste, and since there is no proper logistical infrastructure in most of Sinai, pretty soon the Egyptian troops in the northeast of the peninsula would run out of supplies. At that point they might face an Israeli ground offensive that would encircle and annihilate them. The IDF would also destroy any military infrastructure that might be constructed in Sinai, where such activity is forbidden according to the peace treaty.

Since Israel would probably conduct a giant raid and not a conquest, the IDF would remain in Sinai only until its mission was completed, i.e., destroying Egyptian forces and their sites. Retreating from the peninsula might look to many in the world, mostly the Arab one, like a sign of weakness by Israel, but it might also put a quick end to the war.

Notes

1 Lin Noueihed, *The Battle for the Arab Spring: Revolution, Counter-Revolution and the Making of a New Era* (Yale University Press, 2012), 16.

2 Center for Strategic International Studies (CSIS), March 17, 2014,

http://csis.org/publication/need-new-realism-us-saudi-alliance.

3 Jerusalem Post, May 3, 2014, http://www.jpost.com/Features/Front-Lines/Behind-the-lines-Waging-war-by-other-means-351112.

4 The Washington Post, May 1, 2014, http://www.washingtonpost.com/opinions/robert-kagan-why-the-united-states-shouldnt-support-egypts-ruling-generals/2014/05/01/e7a7403e-d154-11e3-9e25-188ebe1fa93b_story.html.

5 On 2013 see: Gabriel Ben Dor, "Democratization Processes in the Middle East and the Arab World," in *The Arab Spring: Democracy and Security*, ed. Efrain Inbar (New York: Routledge, 2013), 29.

6 The Congressional Research Service (CRS), February 25, 2016, http://www.fas.org/sgp/crs/mideast/RL33003.pdf.

7 CSIS, February 11, 2016, http://csis.org/publication/middle-east-notes-and-comment-egypt-five-years.

8 Tal Nachman, *Islamic Fundamentalism the Case of Egypt and Jordan* (Tel Aviv university, 1999).

9 Besa Center, March 12, 2013, http://besacenter.org/perspectives-papers/egypts-army-will-not-intervene/. USA Today, March 26, 2014, http://www.usatoday.com/story/news/world/2014/03/26/egypt-army-chief-president/6924035/.

10 he Middle East Policy Council, September 9, 2013, http://mepc.org/articles-commentary/commentary/muslim-brotherhood-turning-violence.

11 Middle East Institute, September 12, 2013, http://www.mideasti.org/content/sinai-tipping-point-or-pretext-ouster.

12 Besa Center, March 12, 2013, http://besacenter.org/perspectives-papers/egypts-army-will-not-intervene/.

13 Foreign Affairs, August 20, 2013, http://www.foreignaffairs.com/articles/139835/zack-gold/why-israel-will-miss-morsi.

14 Politico, November 1, 2015, http://www.politico.com/magazine/story/2015/11/sinai-crash-americas-least-known-mideast-military-force-213314#ixzz3qOfCDPdu.

15 Aljazeera, April 11 2014, http://www.aljazeera.com/indepth/features/2014/03/egypt-sinai-caught-middle-201431664729435518.html.

16 Mohannad Sabry, *Sinai: Egypt's Linchpin, Gaza's Lifeline, Israel's Nightmare* (The American University in Cairo Press, 2015). Middle East Institute, February 19, 2015, http://www.mei.edu/content/at/egypts-security-challenge-isis-sinai-and-libyan-border.

17 Al Monitor, May 23, 2014, http://www.al-monitor.com/pulse/en/originals/2014/05/israel-egypt-security-cooperation-netanyahu-livni-nuclear.html.

18 On the heavy handed approach see: The Washington Institute for Near East Policy, January 16, 2014, http://www.washingtoninstitute.org/policy-analysis/view/apaches-in-the-sinai.

19 The Washington Post, June 14, 2015, http://www.washingtonpost.com/opinions/a-strongmans-empty-promise/2015/06/14/c4dca112-111c-11e5-a0dc-2b6f404ff5cf_story.html.

20 The Washington Institute for Near East Policy, May 20, 2015, http://www.washingtoninstitute.org/policy-analysis/view/egypt-two-years-after-morsi.

21 Rubin Center, February 16, 2016, http://www.rubincenter.org/2016/02/between-alliance-and-rivalry-egyptian-israeli-relations-remain-solid-if-not-particularly-warm/.

22 CFR, April 2014, http://www.cfr.org/egypt/egypts-solvency-crisis/p32729.

23 Ynet, July 11, 2016, http://www.ynetnews.com/articles/0,7340,L-4826850,00.html.

24 On the Suez Canal in 2013 see: Foreign Affairs, December 3, 2013, http://www.foreignaffairs.com/articles/140310/steven-a-cook/why-suez-still-matters.

25 Al–Arabiya, November 23, 2014, http://english.alarabiya.net/en/News/middle-east/2014/11/23/Sisi-Egypt-could-send-forces-to-stabilize-future-Palestinian-state.html (accessed March 16, 2016).

26 Daily Mail, July 21, 2016, http://www.dailymail.co.uk/wires/afp/article-3701701/Egypts-Sisi-wants-break-deadlock-peace-process.html.

27 Hossam Eldeen M. Aly, "Prospects for Arms Control in the Middle East," in *Arms Control and Security in the Middle East and The CIS Republics*, eds. Theodore A. Couloumbis, and Thanos P. Dokos (Hellenic Foundation for Europe and Foreign Policy, 1995), 169.

28 Anthony H. Cordesman, *The Military Balance in the Middle East* (London: Praeger, 2004), 137.

29 Steven A. Cook, *The Unspoken Power: Civil-Military Relations and the Prospects for Reform* (Washington, DC: Brookings Institution Press; Project on U.S. Policy towards the Islamic World, 2004), 13.

30 Aljazeera, February 10, 2015, http://www.aljazeera.com/news/2015/02/russia-build-egypt-nuclear-power-plant-150210185343926.html.

31 On the value of Egypt to Saudi Arabia against Iran see: Global Post, August 21, 2013, http://www.globalpost.com/dispatch/news/regions/middle-east/130821/q-why-saudi-arabia-loves-the-egyptian-military.

32 Ehud Eilam, *The Next War between Israel and Egypt—Examining a High Intensity War between Two of the Strongest Militaries in the Middle East* (Edgware, U.K: Vallentine Mitchell, 2014), http://www.amazon.co.uk/The-Next-Between-Israel-Egypt/dp/0853038384.

33 CSIS, June 15, 2015, http://csis.org/files/publication/150615_Nerguizian_Levant_Mil_Bal_Report_w_cover_v2.pdf.

34 On Israeli officers as Rommel see: Hanoch Bartov, *Daddo* (Tel Aviv: Maariv, 1978), vol. 2, 134.

35 Uri Bar-Joseph, "Rotem: The Forgotten Crisis on the Road to the 1967 War," *Journal of Contemporary History* 31 (3) (July 1996): 547-566.

36 Israel National News, June 12, 2014, http://www.israelnationalnews.com/News/News.aspx/188301#.VI8P5CvF-Ck.

37 CSIS, June 15, 2015, http://csis.org/files/publication/150615_Nerguizian_Levant_Mil_Bal_Report_w_cover_v2.pdf.

38 "Egypt's Conventional Military Thinking", Stratfor, June 12, 2015, https://www.stratfor.com/analysis/egypts-conventional-military-thinking.

39 Edward C. Keefer, general ed., *Arab–Israeli Crisis and war, 1973* (Washington, DC: Department of State, United States Government Printing Office, 2011), 693.

40 CSIS, June 15, 2015, http://csis.org/files/publication/150615_Nerguizian_Levant_Mil_Bal_Report_w_cover_v2.pdf.

41 CRS, June 1, 2015, http://www.fas.org/sgp/crs/mideast/RL33476.pdf.

42 On cannibalization see: The New York Times, August 21, 2013, http://www.nytimes.com/2013/08/21/world/middleeast/cairo-military-firmly-hooked-to-us-lifeline.html?_r=0.

43 Christopher O. Bowers, "Identifying Emerging Hybrid Adversaries," *Parameters* (Spring 2012): 47.

44 On the possibility of war with Syria in 2008 see Giora Eiland, "The IDF: Addressing the Failures of the Second Lebanon War," in *The Middle East Strategic Balance 2007–2008*, ed. Mark A. Heller, 35. See also Anthony H. Cordesman with the assistance of Aram Nerguizian and Lonut C. Popescu, *Israel and Syria The Military Balance and Prospects of War* (Westport, CT: Praeger Security International, 2008).

45 John Robb, *Brave New War: The Next Stage of Terrorism and the End of Globalization* (New Jersey: John Wiley & Sons Inc., 2007), 8.

46 The New York Times, August 21, 2013, http://www.nytimes.com/2013/08/21/world/middleeast/cairo-military-firmly-hooked-to-us-lifeline.html?smid=tw-nytimesglobal&seid=auto&_r=1&pagewanted=all&.

47 House Foreign Affairs Committee, Statement for the Record, Honorable Derek Chollet, Assistant Secretary of Defense for International Security Affairs, October 29, 2013, Rayburn 2172, http://iipdigital.usembassy.gov/st/english/texttrans/2013/10/20131029285371.html#ixzz4F4cUGsJr.

48 On jobs in producing tanks in Egypt see: Alarabiya, October 13, 2013, http://english.alarabiya.net/en/perspective/analysis/2013/10/13/Egypt-not-expected-to-be-hit-hard-by-U-S-aid-cuts.html.

49 US Department of State, October 9, 2013, http://www.state.gov/r/pa/prs/ps/2013/10/215258.htm.

50 The New York Times, October 10, 2013, http://www.nytimes.com/2013/10/10/world/middleeast/obama-military-aid-to-egypt.html?_r=0.

51 The New Republic, October 9, 2013, http://www.newrepublic.com/article/115115/obama-cuts-egypt-aid-why-hell-regret-it.

52 On the priorities of Obama see: Brookings, October 15, 2013, http://www.brookings.edu/research/opinions/2013/10/15-american-role-world-ohanlon-shapiro.

53 On the clashes see: The New York Times, October 7, 2013, http://www.nytimes.com/2013/10/07/world/middleeast/clashes-in-egypt-leave-at-least-15-dead.html.

54 On maintenance of AH–64 see: The Washington Institute for Near East Policy, March 4, 2014, http://www.washingtoninstitute.org/policy-analysis/view/egypts-arms-deal-with-russia-potential-strategic-costs.

55 The Washington Institute for Near East Policy, July 8, 2014, http://www.washingtoninstitute.org/policy-analysis/view/u.s.-support-to-counter-egypts-insurgency-still-on-hold.

56 The Guardian, March 31, 2015, http://www.theguardian.com/us-news/2015/mar/31/obama-restores-us-military-aid-to-egypt.

57 Atlantic Council, October 9, 2013, http://www.atlanticcouncil.org/blogs/egyptsource/the-almost-aid-cut-to-egypt.

58 N. Dbory, and A. Rapport, "the IDF in the Next Five Years," *Israel Defense magazine*, (No. three, June–July, 2011), 33–35. On plans for such war see: CSIS, February 10, 2011, http://csis.org/publication/egyptian-military-and-arab-israeli-military-balance see also: Al Monitor, May 22, 2014, http://www.al-monitor.com/pulse/en/originals/2014/05/defense-budget-idf-battle-finance-ministry-welfare-poverty.html.

59 Edward Luttwak, and Dan Horowitz, *The Israeli Army*)New York: Harper and Row Publishers, 1975(, 125. IDF Archive, 56/637/33.

60 On giving most of the budgets to air to air combat see: Walla News, May 22, 2014, http://news.walla.co.il/?w=/2689/2748999.

61 On the F- 35 see: The Times of Israel, April 19, 2015, http://www.timesofisrael.com/could-israeli-f-35s-turn-the-tables-on-iranian-s-300-missiles/.

62 USNews, February 12, 2015, http://www.usnews.com/news/business/articles/2015/02/12/official-egypt-1st-foreign-buyer-of-french-rafale-fighters. http://news.walla.co.il/item/2835362.

63 Al Monitor, February 17, 2016, http://www.al-monitor.com/pulse/en/originals/2016/02/f-35-fighter-jets-israeli-air-force-mig-syrian-skies.html#.

Conclusion

This research examines possible wars or clashes that Israel might face in the near future. Israel's enemies would be in Iran, Lebanon, Syria, the Gaza Strip, the West Bank, and Sinai.

An Israeli raid on Iran

In the late 1970s, Iran became a sworn enemy of Israel, although the two states lack reasons for a conflict. Iran's position is to allow the Israeli Jews to stay where they are as long as they are subordinate to Iran or at least to a pro-Iranian Arab regime. Since Iran opposes Israel's right to exist, having nuclear weapons would enable Iran to reach the declared goal of its leaders: to wipe out Israel.

The July 2015 agreement between Iran and world powers reduced the chances of an Israeli strike on Iran. Yet if the accord is breached, at least from an Israeli perspective, it might bring an Israeli attack against Iran.

Instead of attacking Iran's nuclear infrastructure, Israel might focus on other objectives like the Iranian oil and gas industry. Without it, Iran would lose most of the revenues that keep the nuclear program going. However, smashing Iran's energy infrastructure might destabilize the global oil market and create a worldwide economic crisis, which Israel wishes to avoid. Another Israeli option is to assassinate Iranian leaders or threaten to do that, but the complexity and ramifications of such steps render them too difficult to execute. Israel would probably restrict itself to an attack on the Iranian nuclear infrastructure, abandoning other alternatives.

The Israeli Air Force (IAF), during a raid on Iran, would have to overcome various constraints such as the distance to Iran and

Iranian air defense and fighters. Israeli unmanned aerial vehicle (UAV) could contribute by gathering intelligence and attacking targets. An airborne assault might also be part of the raid. Israel's long-range missiles, those that could be launched from sea or land, would probably be kept for a nuclear showdown.

Once the attack on Iran is launched, Israel would have to warn its whole population and send people to shelters while organizing the country's active and passive defense, among them deploying its antimissile Arrow batteries if Iran fires long-range missiles. The IAF might try to destroy the launchers of Iranian missiles and could also retaliate if needed. Both sides would calculate, according to their casualties and damage on all levels, including the political one, if and how to continue striking each other. They might return to their prolonged cold war, which has been going on since the early 1980s. If Israel attacks Iran, the latter might stick to that kind of conflict and get its revenge by conducting terror attacks against Israeli and/or Jewish objectives worldwide. It could also wait until it gets the bomb.

A Clash with the Hezbollah

Following an Israeli raid on Iran, the latter might retaliate through its proxies near Israel's borders: nonstate organizations such as the Islamic Jihad in the Gaza Strip and particularly the Hezbollah in Lebanon.

The Hezbollah might hesitate, concerned about several aspects: fierce Israeli retribution, heavy criticism from inside Lebanon, and Iran's limited ability to assist the Hezbollah during and after the Israeli attack. Iran would have to allocate a huge budget to rebuild its forces and repair the damage to its infrastructure. Furthermore, if the Hezbollah was badly hit by Israel, and left militarily and politically weak, it would be vulnerable to its enemies in both Lebanon and Syria. Iran might prefer that its Lebanese protégé did not risk itself but waited until Iran has the bomb.

In spite of all that, Hezbollah might very well shoot its rockets. The Israel Defense Forces' (IDF's) strategy would then be to annihilate as many of the rockets as it could, particularly the long-range ones, if possible before they were launched. Although the IDF has overwhelming superiority over the Hezbollah in manpower, weapon systems, etc., a large part of the IAF would focus on Iran, particularly if the raid turned into an exchange of punches that might last for weeks or more. The rest of the Israeli planes and the entire attack helicopter fleet, not having the range to reach Iran, could concentrate on an offensive against the Hezbollah.

Israeli land units not contributing to a collision with Iran would play a major role, if not a decisive one, in the campaign in Lebanon. Therefore, while around a 100 Israeli aircrafts were striking Iran, thousands of different kinds of aircraft, land vehicles, and vessels would be attacking the Hezbollah.

The IDF might launch a full-scale attack deep into Lebanon, as in 1982, but Israel would probably wish to avoid the risks and problems of occupying large parts of Lebanon. Israel was determined in the 2006 war not to go back to the 1980s and the 1990s, since its Lebanese scar was not yet healed. This psychological impediment might continue to hinder Israel in another round in Lebanon. Israel would, therefore, aim at destroying Hezbollah's military infrastructure, mostly its rockets, and collect information and Hezbollah documents. When this task was finished, Israel would retreat to the border.

Tens of thousands of Israeli reserves might be called from their homes to fight in Lebanon after, not before, the raid on Iran in order not to disrupt the element of surprise. It means that the IDF has to train in advance to mobilize its troops under fire, since immediately after the Israeli raid in Iran, the Hezbollah might start to shoot rockets at Israeli cities and bases where the reserves got organized.

The Israeli land offensive inside Lebanon would be based on

infantry, armor, and combat engineers, with close and strong air support and artillery. Boots on the ground would be essential to force Hezbollah's troops out of their shelters so air power could hit them. Israeli land units would also be necessary in cases where the IAF was not able to discover or destroy rockets. Israeli units would capture key sites and crossroads and would try to block the Hezbollah from sending reinforcements and supplies. This maneuver would pave the way to battles on Hezbollah's posts inside villages and towns. It's possible that in some of those places, the local fighters would unofficially allow Israeli ground units a safe passage to the location of the rockets, and in return the IDF would spare the town or village. Other members of the Hezbollah would fight, even to the death. Some of them acquired combat experience in Syria, where they enjoyed support from Assad's aircraft, artillery, and tanks. They would not have this advantage during a war against Israel. Furthermore, the IDF is immeasurably more powerful, protected, and trained than Syrian rebels, against whom the Hezbollah got used to fighting.

Israel aims for a fast decision in order to reduce the cost of war. The number of IDF casualties could rise in a war against the Hezbollah if the battles continue, and the Israeli population would be in great danger if they had to absorb tens of thousands of rockets. The campaign would stretch from Beirut all the way to the south of Israel. The latter's civilian and military infrastructure would be in the range of the rockets and missiles. Hence, Israel's evaluation of the length of the war with the Hezbollah, its success and its cost, would be a major consideration in the debate about whether to bomb Iran or not, since the war with the Hezbollah might be a direct result of that decision.

The Syrian front

From 1974 until recent years, there was total quiet on Israel's border with Syria in the Golan Heights. However, following the civil war in Syria, it was no longer business as usual. In recent years, there were minor assaults against Israel such as mortar shells landing inside the country, to which the IDF responded immediately. This change was reflected in military thinking, which had to switch from the concern since 1974 about a high-intensity war in the Golan Heights to the realization that a low-intensity war in that area was more probable.

In recent years Israel launced air strikes, aiming to prevent the delivery of advanced weapons such as antiaircraft missiles from Syria to the Hezbollah. In order to cause serious disruption of IAF operations, the Hezbollah requires dozens of antiaircraft missile batteries. Currently, the IAF has freedom of action over Lebanon, and this would probably not change during a war against the Hezbollah. Nevertheless, Israel's occasional bombing inside Syria might risk that those strikes would eventually ignite a war with the Hezbollah and/or Syria. In spite of Assad's weakness, he possesses missiles and rockets, including maybe an unconventional arsenal, so Israel has no intention of going to war with him.

Officially, Israel does not support its old enemy Assad. That goes for the rebels as well, particularly since many of them are radical Islamists, who will turn against Israel if they win. In the case of a war between Israel and Assad, Israel could obliterate Assad's best units and by that enable the rebels to topple him. So Israel sees Assad as a kind of buffer against the Islamists, and for this reason, as well as others, Assad and Israel wish to avoid such a confrontation. Unofficially, there has been an Israeli belief that the different parties in Syria should continue to clash with each other as long as possible. It seems Israel has been hoping that the Syrian civil war will be contained within Syria. This wish requires caution on the part of Israel as to its next military steps inside that country, in order to avoid being entangled in a war there. Israel must also think twice about any declaration regarding Syria. However, if an assault from Syria inflicted heavy casualties among Israeli troops and/or civilians, Israel would probably hit back hard.

Assad is an ally of both Iran and the Hezbollah and would be expected to help them during a war between Israel and the Hezbollah and/or Iran. However, Assad might be kept busy in the civil war in Syria and be too weak to participate in a war against Israel.

Syria is almost a failed state and actually exists more as a country where armed forces, groups, and militias struggle with each other. This could go on in the near future, with or without Assad. Israel might have to deal with assaults in the Golan Heights, as in the Gaza Strip. Israel would have to avoid striking back at populated areas inside Syria, even if they served as a springboard for attacks against it. Some of Israel's foes there, particularly those who came from outside Syria, might not care if Syrian civilians were harmed. They might even encourage it for propaganda, using the suffering of the population to incite and gain support and new recruits.

If Assad falls, many weapon systems such as tanks, artillery, antiaircraft missiles, and maybe also chemical weapons (CW) will end up in the hands of all kinds of groups. Israel and other states, mostly Western ones, should strive to destroy weapon systems that could be used against them or their allies. If Syria as a state ceases to exist, there will be no local air force or coordinated air defense that could shoot down Israeli and Western aircraft conducting missions like reconnaissance and bombardments across that war-torn country. Besides blowing up Syrian weapon systems, Israel might intercept in the air and bomb on the ground Iranian supplies on their way to Iran's protégés in Syria and Lebanon. Those Israeli assaults might ignite a confrontation between Israel and Iran. Israel might also send its planes to bomb Iran through the open skies of Syria and Iraq.

The Alawites, particularly if the Assad regime crumbles, would lose much of their power and might be pinned down to areas near the shorelines, far from the Israeli border and not much of a concern to Israel. The latter would focus on other areas, mostly those near the Golan Heights. Israel has already given humanitarian aid to about 2,000 Syrians and might collaborate with Syrian Sunnis,

Druze, and Christians, against their common enemies: radical Islamists. Israel, Western powers, and Jordan might provide their Syrian allies with weapons, information, and training while sticking to air strikes and avoiding boots on the ground.

Hamas

There is a fierce struggle inside Palestinian society between the Palestinian Authority (PA) and the Hamas. Israel and the PA have had their times of friction and skirmishes, but there have also been periods of negotiations. Israel's relationship with the Hamas has been more hostile in spite of mutual understandings over the years.

The PA controlled most of the Gaza Strip in 1994–2005 and all of it in 2005–2007. From 2007, the Hamas took over the Gaza Strip, and Israel has been cooperating with the PA against the Hamas in the West Bank.

Israel, with or without aid from the PA, could conquer all the Gaza Strip quite fast, due to its overwhelming military superiority and the vulnerability of the Gaza Strip, which has no strategic depth or natural obstacles to stop an attacker. The Hamas for its part would strive to inflict as many casualties as possible on the IDF and to slow down its advance. Israel could topple the Hamas and pave the way for the PA to regain its hold over the Gaza Strip. The PA, however, might refuse to be seen as returning to power in the Gaza Strip by depending on the IDF, although the PA's survival in the West Bank is to a large extent due to the deployment of the IDF there. Even if the PA takes over the Gaza Strip, it might not manage to hold its ground there. Israel would probably not want to join, let alone replace, the PA in running the Gaza Strip because of political, military, and economic constraints.

The Hamas, fearing an Israeli offensive, was sometimes willing to limit and even stop its attacks against Israel and restrain other guerrilla and terror groups in the Gaza Strip from provoking Israel. One of them is the Islamic Jihad, which, in addition to its strong devotion to its anti-Israel ideology, might try to manipulate Israel into attacking its rival, the Hamas. This could open the way for the Islamic Jihad to take over the Gaza Strip. Iran, having been a patron of the Islamic Jihad, might strive to topple the Hamas, following the rift between them, and have the Islamic Jihad replace Hamas as rulers of the Gaza Strip. Such a move would enable Iran to turn the Gaza Strip into a base against Israel in case the latter strikes Iran.

Iran's major allies, Assad and the Hezbollah, did not support the Hamas against Israel in the confrontations in 2008–2009 and in 2012 and 2014. In 2012 and 2014, it made sense because by then the Hamas was not in their camp. This was not the case in 2008–2009, but Iran and its allies chose not to stand by the Hamas at that time.

Egypt has a complicated relationship with the Palestinians, including ruling over them and using them against Israel in the mid-1950s, serving as a broker between them and Israel since the 1990s, and allowing the smuggling of weapons and ammunitions from Sinai to the Gaza Strip for more than a decade. Only in recent years has Egypt finally made a serious effort to stop the smuggling from Sinai. If this activity resumes, Israel might try to stop it by seizing part of the Gaza Strip, near the border with Sinai, or by going further inside the Gaza Strip in order to prevent direct friction with Egypt.

In spite of the current tension and hostility between Egypt and the Hamas, a major clash between Israel and the Hamas might entangle Egypt in it against its will. Iran considers Egypt a strategic rival in the struggle for hegemony in the region. Iran might push the pro-Iranian Islamic Jihad to provoke Israel in order to fire up a confrontation between not just Israel and the Hamas but between Israel and Egypt as well. Such a war would weaken two of Iran's biggest enemies in the Middle East and would divert attention away from the Iranian nuclear project.

In the years before the 2014 confrontation, there were many

skirmishes near the fence that surrounds the Gaza Strip. The Israeli defense was quite effective there, so the Hamas resorted to digging tunnels under the border fence and shooting rockets and mortar shells above it. Israel used aircraft to strike launchers and/or their crew. Such friction might ignite another confrontation such as a preventive war or a preemptive strike by Israel against the Hamas, but such an attack e would most likely take place as a response to a deadly assault on Israel form the Gaza Strip.

In the West Bank, the lack of talks between Israel and the PA increases the chances of deterioration into a wave of violent demonstrations, with or without the support of the PA. Either way the situation might escalate, particularly if there are a lot of casualties among the Palestinians, which would make the struggle look more and more like a low-intensity war, as in 2000–2005.

A future clash between Israel and Egypt

There are several factors that might cause considerable tension between Israel and Egypt, possibly leading to a major crisis. In the worst case, it might even end in a clash against the will of one or both sides.

Israel hopes that Egypt will focus on its substantial economic and political problems without diverting the public's attention toward Israel by blaming it for Egypt's serious troubles. Israel and Egypt deal with armed groups in Sinai that pose a threat to both Israel and Egypt. The latter may also harbor an ulterior motive: seeking to end the demilitarization of Sinai, one of the most basic components of the 1979 peace treaty. Egypt has been changing the situation de facto, ever since Israel allowed Egypt to reinforce its units in Sinai. This process, whereby Egypt uses its troops to suppress guerilla and terror groups, might undermine the peace treaty. Meanwhile, one assault from Sinai might inflict considerable losses on Israelis. In response, Israel might threaten to or actually openly retaliate inside Sinai, which Egypt would strongly oppose. Other causes for friction between Israel and Egypt might be a violent collision between Israel and the Palestinians and ongoing issues like Israel's nuclear program.

A clash between Israel and Egypt could be a devastating experience that Egypt, Israel, and the United States should try to prevent before it is too late. The United States could assist in this matter by adjusting its aid to Egypt and training the Egyptian military to win a low-intensity war in Sinai before this conflict turns Israel and Egypt against each other. The United States, with Saudi's help, should also assist Egypt in developing the civilian infrastructure in Sinai, such as by creating jobs, which might reduce the motivation of the local population there to support guerrilla and terror groups.

A confrontation between Israel and Egypt would test the performance of their militaries in a high-intensity war. The buildup of each side before the battles would play a decisive role. In recent years, the IDF has been training mostly against hybrid foes like the Hezbollah and the Hamas, along with exercising for a strike on the Iranian nuclear sites. This came at the expense of preparing for a war against Egypt. The IDF might also rely too much on the IAF, although the latter might be able to gain quick air superiority and then destroy Egyptian ground units. Much would depend on where Egypt deployed its forces, whether near the border with Israel, which would extend Egypt's supply lines, or close to the Suez Canal, relatively near Egypt's main bases.

All in all, given the degree of tension in the Middle East, Israel might wind up in an armed confrontation on one or more of its borders. It seems that preparations should be directed above all at confronting Israel's most powerful hybrid foe, the Hezbollah. The fight against the Hezbollah would focus on reducing the firing of rockets on Israel's rear.

In Syria, Israel might fight Islamist groups. In the case of a confrontation in the Gaza Strip and/or in the West Bank, Israel has to decide whether to recapture parts or even all of the West Bank/

Gaza Strip and whether to topple Palestinian rule there. Israel might also be entangled in a severe crisis and in the worst case in a clash with Egypt, mostly following the lawlessness in Sinai and the instability inside Egypt.

From a political point of view, Israel could try to avoid or postpone a confrontation by signing a new peace agreement with the PA and by keeping the current one with Egypt.

Israel should have at least a mutual understanding with the PA and Egypt, formal or not, if only pertaining to security aspects. Israel should consider doing the same with Assad, the rebels in Syria, the Hamas, the Hezbollah, and even Iran. At the same time, Israel has to continue to prepare for confrontations with all those states and nonstate organizations. The IDF needs to deter them from harming Israel and if necessary to confront them, including by launching massive and/or sudden attacks. The IDF should concentrate on hybrid foes, primarily the Hezbollah, but without neglecting its ability to run a high-intensity war against potential rivals like Egypt. Israel has to be ready to handle all its fronts since a clash, minor or major, might happen in each of those fronts in the upcoming years and actually anytime now.

Further Reading

Abrahms, Max. (2006) Why Terrorism Does Not Work. *International Security* 31 (2): 42-78.

Adamsky, D. (2010) *The Culture of Military Innovation*. Stanford University Press.

Amit, M. (1990) *Head On*. Or Yehuda: Had Arzi.

Alpher, Yossi. (2015) *Periphery—Israel's Search for Middle East Allies*. Rowman & Littlefield Publishers.

Beres, Louis René. (2016) *Surviving Amid Chaos: Israel's Nuclear Strategy*. Lanham, MD: Rowman & Littlefield.

Brown, N. (1986) *The Future of Air Power*. London: Croom Helm.

Cohen, A.S. (1994) How did the "Intifada" affect the IDF? *Conflict Quarterly* 14 (3): 7–22.

Cordesman, A.H. (2002) *Peace and War: The Arab–Israeli Military Balance Enters the 21st Century*. London: Praeger.

Dupuy, T.N. (1978) *Elusive Victory*. London: Macdonald and Janes.

Gamasy El, G. A. M. (1993) *The October War*. The American University in Cairo.

Gellber, Y. (2004) The Israeli–Arab War of 1948: History Versus Narratives. In *A Never Ending Conflict—A Guide To Israeli Military History*, ed. M. Bar, 43-68. London: Praeger.

Golan, S. (2007) *A War on Three Fronts*. Tel Aviv: Ministry of Defense.

Inbar, E., ed. 2007. *Israel's Strategic Agenda*. London and New York: Routledge.

Inbar, E. and S. Sandler. (1993/4) Israel's Deterrence Strategy Revisited. *Security Studies* 3 (2): 330–358.

Kam, E. (1990) *Surprise Attack*. Tel Aviv: Maarachot.

Kreis, J.F. (2002) *Air Warfare and Air Base Air Defense 1914–1973*. Honolulu, HI: University Press of the Pacific.

Lieberman, E. (1995) What Makes Deterrence Work? Lessons from the Egyptian–Israeli Enduring Rivalry. *Security Studies* 4 (Summer): 851–910.

Pollack, K.M. (2004) *Arabs at War*. Lincoln, NE: University of Nebraska Press.

Rabinovich, I. (2011) *The View from Damascus: State, Political Community and Foreign Relations in Twentieth-Century Syria*. Edgware, UK: Vallentine Mitchell.

Sakal, E. (2011) *"The Regulars will Hold!"?—The Missed Opportunity to Prevail in the Defensive Campaign in Western Sinai in the Yom Kippur War*. Tel Aviv: Ma'ariv Book Guild.

Shamir, E. (2011) *Transforming Command*. Stanford, CA: Stanford University Press.

Shimshi, E. (1995) *By Virtue of Stratagem*. Tel Aviv: Ministry of Defense.

Tamir, A. (1988) *A Soldier in Search of Peace*. Tel Aviv: Edanim.

Weizman, E. (1981) *The Battle for Peace*. Jerusalem: Edanim.

Yonay, E. (1995) *No Margin for Error*. Jerusalem: Ketr.

Yzaki, S. (1969) *In The Eyes of the Arabs*. Tel Aviv: Ministry of Defense.

19716049R00099

Printed in Great Britain
by Amazon